Riddles in a Language Arts Classroom

Cloud Kingdom Games

Steve Martin

Contributors & Editors:

Robin Marks
Blake Montana
Vicky Mayfield
Rick Smith
Rod Stephens

ISBN 978-1-928807-19-3

Shelve under Parenting & Education - Education - Teaching Reference

Riddles in a Language Arts Classroom:

A Resource Book for Teachers

"Who wants to solve a riddle?" This question is liable to get a more enthusiastic response from many students than "Who wants to read a poem?" This resource book is designed to make the study of poetic conventions more enjoyable for the students. Riddles invite the use of higher order thinking skills in arriving at their solutions.

The riddles in this book can be used simply as brain teasers. Try posting a riddle for students to mull over each Monday morning. The included student worksheets can provide some necessary scaffolding for students who may need their thinking guided in solving a riddle. The pages marked "For the Teacher" provide teachable features of each riddle poem. These list aspects for the study of poetry.

The Index will become helpful when trying to match the objective of a lesson with the particular poems in this volume. If, for example, you need to teach a lesson about metaphor, you can simply scan the Index under "metaphor" to find the page numbers of riddles that exemplify this trait. A review of the quick notes on the corresponding teacher page will make class preparation very simple.

Poetic riddles are a centuries old tradition in English having their birth in the oral tradition. Riddles in the oral tradition are now known as folk riddles, and they share certain conventions including rhyme and meter. Often these riddles do not translate well to other cultures (and especially other languages) because peculiarities of the place and time engender specific clues that are lost outside of that society.

Eventually scholars sat down at the writing desk to craft poetic riddles, the resulting efforts are now called literary riddles. Sometimes a distinction is made based on the theme of the riddle. Where the folk riddle tends to mask everyday objects, the literary riddle tends to deal more in the realm of abstract ideas. For this volume, it is enough to know that riddles can be both read and heard. Some riddles will have a better effect if they are read aloud. Others depend on the written form to provide all the clues.

Each of the thirty riddles in this book is an original work written by poets associated with Cloud Kingdom Games. This company has produced hundreds of original riddles many of which are available in a series of riddle books (see the inside back cover of this volume). Although the form of these riddles spring from a long tradition of riddling in English, typically, today's students have little experience with this form of entertainment. Those that they may have come across in nursery rhymes are not presented as riddles. (Indeed the answer is often pictured alongside the riddle in children's books.) And so the students miss the fun of figuring them out.

One purpose of this volume is to help reintroduce poetic riddles to the students of today. This volume is meant as a vehicle to get at some of the fun aspects of using language to hide the truth in plain sight.

Contents

Each lesson has two parts, the Instructor's copy and the Student worksheet.

Copies of the Student worksheets are also available online at: www.CloudKingdom.com/RIALAC.

For the Teacher

Riddle Title: **Never Orange**

I'm never orange,/Though yellow can be./A bard's good friend,/In his songs you find me./In a child's book kept,/And in ballads too,/I'll bet you're surprised/Not to find me right here.

The answer to this riddle is: <u>**Rhyme**</u>

This riddle has the following teachable feature: Rhyme

Rhyme—a repetition of similar sounds in two or more words most often used in poetry and songs.

This riddle can be used in the classroom to introduce a discussion of the power of rhyme in English verse. You will find that most students do not have a particularly difficult time solving this riddle. Why not? A student explanation of *how* they solved this riddle is an excellent starting point. The gimme clue is in the last two lines: "I'll bet you're surprised not to find me right here." This very short poem managed to set up in the listener a full expectation of a rhyming last word. The missing rhyme is an obvious, if ironic, clue to the riddle's answer. But how did the poet set up this strong expectation in such a short verse?

The first place to look is at the one rhyme (be/me) that DOES function in the verse. This, of course, is the set-up. The listener, while the poem is being read, develops the full expectation that this verse will behave as two quatrains each with the rhyme scheme abcb. The fact that the second quatrain misbehaves is a shock. How does this work?

Is the *rhythm* driving the listener to expect the rhyme? Maybe. But the rhythm in this poem is fairly choppy. A case could be made that the odd lines (1,3, 5, and 7) are typically shorter with two stressed syllables each, and the (typically longer) even lines also have two stressed syllables each; therefore a certain inevitability is set up rhythmically. But it is not the whole story. Consider this mutated limerick:

> *There once was a man from Siam*
> *Whose poems got way out of hand.*
> *When he was asked why,*
> *He merely replied,*
> *Because I try to get as many words into the last line as ever I possibly can.*

In this example, the poet shocks the listener by violating a well established rhythmic structure while maintaining the expected rhyme scheme (with near rhymes).

There is no doubt that most students hearing "Never Orange" will expect a rhyme at the end. If we cannot fully credit the rhythmic structure for setting up this expectation, then there must be another contributing factor. Either the expectation is built on familiarity with structured verse that does not violate this rule, or, the student is somehow hardwired to recognize and pick up rhyming patterns in language naturally. If the second hypothesis is true, then bards, songwriters, poets, and teachers can be opportunists who take advantage of this natural predisposition.

In the English oral tradition, songs, ballads, verses, and riddles have been built with rhyme as a key component. The rhyme functions to make the words memorable, just like the words of a song that gets stuck in one's head. When trying to remember lyrics, sometimes the easiest parts to remember are the rhyming words, and they can help one reconstruct some of what remains. As a study tool, rhyme can be a great mnemonic device. With a little creativity, students can invent a rhyme to help them remember key points in a lesson no matter the topic.

Teacher copy of student worksheet

This reference page is designed to show you what the student worksheet looks like.

Sample answers are provided in italics.

<u>Never Orange</u>

I'm never orange,
Though yellow can be.
A bard's good friend,
In his songs you find me.

In a child's book kept,
And in ballads too,
I'll bet you're surprised
Not to find me right here.

Figuring it out!

This is an "I am" riddle where the speaker is the answer to the riddle. The job of the solver is to figure out what the "I" is that is speaking the riddle. It is not a person.

Complete the items below:

1. A bard is the same as a poet. Bards of old would sing or recite epic or heroic poetry. Imagine that a bard was singing to you. What kinds of things might you find in his songs? In the space below write down as many features of songs as you can think of.
melody, verses, chorus, story, rhyme, rhythm, music, love themes

2. The answer to this riddle, whatever it is, is kept in a child's book. Children's books have some typical features. In the space below write down a list of features that are common in books for very young children.
illustrations, bright colors, nursery rhymes, funny stories, fables

3. A ballad is a simple song that tells a story. Ballads usually have a melody line that repeats as the story is told. There are many popular songs that are called ballads like "American Pie" and "The Ballad of Billy the Kid." Imagine that you were asked to write a ballad.   In the space below, write a list of things you would be sure to include in your ballad.
a story, a repeating melody line, a chorus, verses, a good beat, etc...

4. The last lines of this riddle say" I'll bet your surprised not to find me right here." Given your answers to the questions above, what might one expect to find at the end of the last line that is missing?
a rhyming word.

5. Did you figure it out?

   If so, what is the answer to this riddle? _______ *Rhyme* _______

For the Teacher

Riddle Title: **Shooting Rays**

Rays shoot from its heart/Spoke silently without words/Fastest when tired.

The answer to this riddle is: <u>**Wheel**</u>

This riddle has the following teachable features: Personification, Irony, Pun and Haiku

Personification—a descrption of something inanimate as being a living person or animal.

In this riddle the answer, "wheel," is an inanimate object. However it is being personified in all the following ways. It has a "heart." And (if the poem is misinterpreted as the poet intends) the wheel also speaks, and it gets tired (as in fatigued). These examples show the poet's use of personification as a vehicle for misdirection which is, after all, one major goal of the riddle.

Irony—an incongruity or discordance that goes strikingly beyond the most simple and evident meaning of words. It is sometimes the deliberate use of language that states the direct opposite of the truth.

 In this short riddle, irony abounds. The seeming oxymoronic "Spoke silently" gives a surface-level irony. The last line, "Fastest when tired", also has an ironic effect on the listener who pays attention to the most simple and evident meaning of the words. It is not often that the fatigued runner is the fastest one in the race for example.

Pun— is a form of word play that deliberately exploits ambiguity between similar-sounding words for humorous or rhetorical effect.

In this riddle, the following words function as puns for the purpose of misdirection: spoke, and tired. The listener will think of "spoke" in terms of speaking, before thinking of the spoke of a wheel. The listener, too, is likely to think of "tired" as fatigued before thinking of it in terms of a tire of a bicycle, car or some other vehicle.

Haiku— is a form of poetry (originally Japanese) consisting of 17 syllables in three metrical phrases of 5, 7, and 5 respectively.

This riddle follows the syllable structure of haiku. In English, haiku are generally broken into three lines by syllable count. The first line –Rays/shoot/from/its/heart—is five syllables. The second line—Spoke/si/lent/ly/with/out/words—is seven syllables. The third line—Fast/est/when/ti/red—is five syllables. (The last word "tired" is sometimes considered to be a one-syllable word except that the diphthong makes it sound like two as in "tahy-rd").

In its pure Japanese form, haiku typically require two additional elements. One is a seasonal reference (kigo). The other is a "cutting word" (kirji). Sometimes this kriji acts to point out the similarities between two different thoughts in the poem. While difficult to translate into English, it might be helpful to think of the kirji as making the verse function metaphorically.

In Japan, the poet Bashō is rightly credited with raising the haiku genre from a playful witty game to a high form of poetry. (Similarly the riddle genre in English can be both witty and poetic.) Famous throughout the world, Bashō's work has eventually resulted in worldwide popularity of the haiku as a verse form.

Extra Activity—Have your students write haiku experimentally by following the structure of haiku poetry in English. They can try to write a verse that simply follows these rules. Write exactly three lines with the 5, 7, 5 syllable count. Advanced students can incorporate kigo and kirji. Alternatively advanced students can try to write a haiku riddle.

Teacher copy of student worksheet
This reference page is designed to show you what the student worksheet looks like.
Sample answers are provided in italics.

Shooting Rays

Rays shoot from its heart
Spoke silently without words
Fastest when tired.

Figuring it out!

Complete the items below:

1. This riddle is only three lines long, but that does not mean it is easy to solve. In the first line "Rays shoot from its heart" the word "heart" does not mean the beating machine that pumps blood in a person or an animal. Think of other meanings of the word heart and write them in the space below.
   the center of a thing, the core, the main idea, spirit of an athlete

2. The phrase "rays shoot" begins the first line of this riddle, but this is not some kind of death ray that someone is shooting. There are other meanings to the word "rays" apart from the sun's rays, or laser beams. Furthermore these" rays" are not intended to be aimed at anyone or shot at anyone. In the space below, write other possible meanings of the phrase "rays shoot."
   arms and legs splay, ribs hamg, ropes surround, lines emanate

3. The word "spoke" in the second line does not refer to someone who was talking. Can you think of anything else that could be meant by the word spoke? In the space below write down any other meanings of the word spoke that you can think of.
   the spoke in a bicycle, an umbrella spoke, the rung of a ladder

4. The word "tired" in the third line does not refer to fatigue. It has nothing to do with being exhausted at all. Can you think of any other meanings for the word tired? Write them down in the space below.
   a stale joke, a car's tires, a bicycle's tires, dressed up, run over

5. Did you figure it out? If so, what is the answer to this riddle?

   Answer: ______*Wheel*______

For the Teacher

Riddle Title: **The Oracle**

> Eastern oracle/Conceals the future within/A light and sweet cave.

The answer to this riddle is: <u>**Fortune cookie**</u>

This riddle has the following teachable features: Irony, Metaphor, and Haiku

Irony—an incongruity or discordance that goes strikingly beyond the most simple and evident meaning of words. It is sometimes the deliberate use of language that states the direct opposite of the truth.

Oracles are generally considered to be wise and prophetic. An exotic "eastern oracle," the listener can assume, is probably an extremely venerable example of this. Fortune cookie fortunes, on the other hand, contain statements that are generally considered to be far from accurate. These "fortunes" are more of a game than a serious attempt at predicting the future. Once the riddle is solved, the ironic idea that a fortune cookie is the hiding place for an accurate prediction from some mystical oracular power from the Far East is revealed. On solving the riddle, then, the irony becomes obvious.

Metaphor—expressing one thing in terms normally denoting another.

This riddle implies that a fortune cookie is a cave. Caves are large, dark places with narrow openings. On a smaller scale, one can see the similarities between this and the inside of a fortune cookie. Caves are not generally considered to be "light" and "sweet" however, so these words serve to point out the differences between an actual cave and this metaphorical one. These differences become necessary hints for the correct solution. This riddle, without these key words (Eastern oracle conceals the future within a cave) becomes much harder to solve.

Haiku— is a form of poetry (originally Japanese) consisting of 17 syllables in three metrical phrases of 5, 7, and 5 respectively.

This riddle follows the syllable structure of haiku. In English, haiku are generally broken into three lines by syllable count. The first line –East/ern/or/a/cle—is five syllables. The second line—Con/ceals/the/fu/ture/with/in—is seven syllables. The third line—A/light/and/sweet/cave—is five syllables.

In its pure Japanese form, haiku typically require two additional elements. One is a seasonal reference (kigo). The other is a "cutting word" (kirji). Sometimes this kriji acts to point out the similarities between two different thoughts in the poem. While difficult to translate into English, it might be helpful to think of the kirji as making the verse function metaphorically. In this riddle the word "cave" acts as a kirji.

In Japan, the poet Bashō is rightly credited with raising the haiku genre from a playful witty game to a high form of poetry. (Similarly the riddle genre in English can be both witty and poetic.) Famous throughout the world, Bashō's work has eventually resulted in worldwide popularity of the haiku as a verse form.

Extra Activity—Have your students write haiku experimentally by following the structure of haiku poetry in English. They can try to write a verse that simply follows these rules. Write exactly three lines with the 5, 7, 5 syllable count. Advanced students can incorporate kigo and kirji. Alternatively advanced students can try to write a haiku riddle.

Teacher copy of student worksheet

This reference page is designed to show you what the student worksheet looks like.

Sample answers are provided in italics.

The Oracle

Eastern oracle
Conceals the future within
A light and sweet cave.

Figuring it out!

Complete the items below:

1. This riddle is only three lines long, but that does not mean it is easy to solve. The first line "Eastern oracle" contains the word oracle. An oracle is a person or place that is a source of wise counsel and accurate predictions of the future. Palm readers and Ouija boards are considered by some to be modern oracles. In the space below, write out a list of things that are supposed to be able to predict the future.
   fortune-teller, gypsy, the futures market, science fiction, etc...

2. The word cave evokes images of a dark place where things can hide (or be hidden). Caves are not generally thought of as "light" and "sweet," but the cave in the riddle is described as both. In the spaces below, list things that are light in weight, and then things that are sweet.
   Light—feathers, paper, sawdust, powder, meringue, leaves, pollen
   Sweet—cookies, cakes, honey, sugar, chocolate, gummy bears,

3. The answer to this riddle is something that hides (conceals) the future in a light and sweet and dark place (cave). Suppose you knew the future, and you wanted to hide what you knew in something light and sweet. In the space below describe what you would do.
   I would write the future in a message, wrap it in a fireproof, heatproof container, and put it inside some cake dough. Then I would cook the cake and serve it. The message about the future would be hidden inside.

4. Did you figure it out? If so, what is the answer to this riddle?

   Answer: _____ *Fortune cookie* _____

For the Teacher

Riddle Title: **The Traveler**

> Travels by whispers/Or else its death is certain/Passageway concealed

The answer to this riddle is: <u>**Secret**</u>

This riddle has the following teachable features: Personification and Haiku

Personification—a description of something inanimate as being a living person or animal.

In this riddle the answer, "secret" is a concept or idea. However it is being treated with some of the attributes of living things. Not only does it travel, but it can also die.

Haiku— is a form of poetry (originally Japanese) consisting of 17 syllables in three metrical phrases of 5, 7, and 5 respectively.

This riddle follows the syllable structure of haiku. In English, haiku are generally broken into three lines by syllable count. The first line –tra/vels/by/whis/pers—is five syllables. The second line—Or/else/its/death/is/cer/tain—is seven syllables. The third line—Pass/age/way/con/cealed—is five syllables.

In its pure Japanese form, haiku typically require two additional elements. One is a seasonal reference (kigo). The other is a "cutting word" (kirji). Sometimes this kriji acts to point out the similarities between two different thoughts in the poem. While difficult to translate into English, it might be helpful to think of the kirji as making the verse function metaphorically.

In Japan, the poet Bashō is rightly credited with raising the haiku genre from a playful witty game to a high form of poetry. (Similarly the riddle genre in English can be both witty and poetic.) Famous throughout the world, Bashō's work has eventually resulted in worldwide popularity of the haiku as a verse form.

Extra Activity—Have your students write haiku experimentally by following the structure of haiku poetry in English. They can try to write a verse that simply follows these rules. Write exactly three lines with the 5, 7, 5 syllable count. Advanced students can incorporate kigo and kirji. Alternatively advanced students can try to write a haiku riddle.

Bonus Riddle—The haiku riddle below may be amusing to those of your students familiar with the concept of using footnotes.

Toe Tunes

Like tunes from your toe
Words that don't upset the flow
Look up then below.*

* The answer to the Bonus Riddle is *footnote*.

The Traveler

Travels by whispers
Or else its death is certain
Passageway concealed

Figuring it out!

Complete the items below:

1. This riddle is made up of two different clues. The first clue is in the first two lines. Whatever the answer to this riddle is, it is a thing that can only travel by whispers or else it is sure to be destroyed. In the space below write down things you would need to whisper:

   surprises birthday parties, things you say in church, secrets

2. The second clue is in the third line. It says passageway concealed. This clue is a slightly different way to think about the one-word answer to this riddle. In the space below write as many different words you can think of that mean the same thing as the word "concealed."

   wrapped up, under wraps, hidden, pocketed, secreted, put away

   Look at what you just wrote for both numbers one and two above. Are there any words that are on both your lists?

3. Did you figure it out? If so, what is the answer to this riddle?

   Answer: _______ *Secret* _______

For the Teacher

Riddle Title: **Friendly Ghost**

Ghostly companion!/Flat black mirror of your soul./Partner eternal.

The answer to this riddle is: **Shadow**

This riddle has the following teachable features: Personification, Metaphor, Assonance and Haiku

Personification—a description of something inanimate as being a living person or animal.

In this riddle the answer, "shadow" (though it often appears to move) is actually inanimate. Its movements are always attributable to outside forces, and are never an intrinsic decision. However it is being personified by being given the features of a companion, and also those of a loyal partner. Also, because it is "ghostly" it is seen as sharing some of the same features as a ghost. A shadow can take the shape of a person, is insubstantial, and yet appears to move. Sometimes a shadow can even appear to move with intent.

Metaphor—expressing one thing in terms normally denoting another.

This riddle claims that a shadow is a companion, a partner, and a mirror. Like a companion, your shadow is often with you even walking alongside you. And like a partner, it often seems to be engaged in the same activities as you are. It goes to the same meetings, works and plays on your schedule. Like a mirror, your shadow reflects your image and your movements, but it lacks dimensionality and color so it is a flat black mirror.

Assonance—a refrain of vowel sounds to create internal rhyming within phrases.

In the middle line, the words "Flat black" is a crisp example of assonance.

Haiku— is a form of poetry (originally Japanese) consisting of 17 syllables in three metrical phrases of 5, 7, and 5 respectively.

This riddle follows the syllable structure of haiku. In English, haiku are generally broken into three lines by syllable count. The first line –Ghost/ly/com/pan/ion—is five syllables. The second line—Flat/black/mir/ror/of/your/soul—is seven syllables. The third line—Part/ner/e/tern/al—is five syllables.

In its pure Japanese form, haiku typically require two additional elements. One is a seasonal reference (kigo). The other is a "cutting word" (kirji). Sometimes this kriji acts to point out the similarities between two different thoughts in the poem. While difficult to translate into English, it might be helpful to think of the kirji as making the verse function metaphorically. In this riddle, the word "soul" might be considered a kirji because it invites the hearer to think about one's shadow as reflecting the spiritual self and not merely the physical self.

In Japan, the poet Bashō is rightly credited with raising the haiku genre from a playful witty game to a high form of poetry. (Similarly the riddle genre in English can be both witty and poetic.) Famous throughout the world, Bashō's work has eventually resulted in worldwide popularity of the haiku as a verse form.

Extra Activity—Have your students write haiku experimentally by following the structure of haiku poetry in English. They can try to write a verse that simply follows these rules. Write exactly three lines with the 5, 7, 5 syllable count. Advanced students can incorporate kigo and kirji. Alternatively advanced students can try to write a haiku riddle.

Friendly Ghost

Ghostly companion!
Flat black mirror of your soul.
Partner eternal.

Figuring it out!

Complete the items below:

1. The answer to this short riddle is one word. All parts of this riddle describe one thing. It is described as both a companion and a partner. In the space below write down all the qualities that you find in a companion, and then the qualities you find in a partner. This will help you discover some qualities shared by the answer to this riddle, so do not worry if some of the words on these two lists are the same.

   Companion →   *always with you, shares your experiences, friendly*

   Partner →works with you on the same jobs, teammate, lab partner

2. Mirrors are funny things. They enable you to see things you cannot touch, taste, hear, or smell. In the space below write a description of what you would see in a mirror if you crossed a room while looking at it.

   I would see an image of myself crossing the room.

3. The answer to this riddle is also described as ghostly. In the space below write down as many qualities of a ghost as you can think of.

   invisible, insubstantial, haunting, won't leave, intangible, scary

4. The ghost in this riddle is different from the white ghosts one might see on Halloween. This ghost is described as both black and flat. Imagine a black ghost walking around that is also as flat as a pancake! In the space below, write down a list of things that are both flat and black.

   a spatula, the surface of an oil slick, a stovetop, a shadow

5. So, we have something that is like a companion and loyal partner that shares some qualities of a mirror, and is a flat black ghost. Did you figure it out? If so, what is the answer to this riddle?

Answer: *Shadow*

For the Teacher

Riddle Title: **By the Road**

Board by the road/On the face of a duck/A check is now due/Folded, where cash is stuck

The answer to this riddle is: **Bill**

This riddle has the following teachable features: Homonym, Rhyme, and Meter.

Homonym—one of a group of words that share the same spelling *and* the same pronunciation but have different meanings

The answer to this riddle is a homonym. The poet hints at the different meanings of the homonym in the different lines of the riddle. A "bill" is a part of a duck's face. But it is also a way for a lender to indicate that a debt is due. It is also something you stick in a billfold. And it is an advertisement that you post, perhaps on a billboard.

This riddle might be a good introduction to the concept of a *homonym* for your students.

Rhyme—a repetition of similar sounds in two or more words most often used in poetry and songs.

This riddle has the following end-of-line rhymes: duck/stuck. The rhyme scheme is *abcb*.

Meter—is the basic rhythmic structure of a verse.

Anapest—consists of two short syllables followed by a long one.

This short riddle, while not consistent throughout, might be a good introduction to the use of the anapest as a metrical foot. An anapest is a metrical foot of three beats, the first two being unstressed, and the third stressed. The second line of this riddle is made up of two anapests.

One way to express this is:

da	da	DUM	da	da	DUM
On	the	face	of	a	duck

In this riddle, the following metrical feet are anapests: /by the road/on the face/of a duck/is now due.

A familiar poem with a regular anapestic rhythm is "The Night Before Christmas" by Clement Clarke Moore or Henry Livingston. Consider these first few lines. The stress is indicated by bolding.

'Twas the **night** before **Chris**tmas when **all** through the **house**

Not a **Crea**ture was **stir**ring not **even** a **mouse**.

Teacher copy of student worksheet
This reference page is designed to show you what the student worksheet looks like.
Sample answers are provided in italics.

By the Road

Board by the road
On the face of a duck
A check is now due
Folded, where cash is stuck

Figuring it out!

Complete the items below:

1. The answer to this riddle is a word that has multiple meanings. The clues in this puzzle hint at the different meanings of the word. The first line "Board by the road" is hinting at one meaning of the answer. In the space below, list as many kinds of "boards" as you can think of. Especially think about "boards" that you can see from the road.
   sign board, board fence, billboard, snowboard, skateboard

2. The second line talks about the face of a duck. In the box below see if you can draw the face of a duck.

Can you name the different parts of the face?
List the parts of a duck's face here:
   Eyes
   Bill
   Feathers

3. The third line says that "A check is now due." This means that someone needs to write a check in order to pay a debt. What do you pay with a check? Can you think of words associated with writing checks? List them below;
   checkbook, bill, bank, teller, sign, write, balance, debt, pay

4. The last line says "Folded where cash is stuck." In the space below, write a list of places where people keep their cash? Can you think of one that contains the word "fold"?
   purse, pocket, wallet, billfold, clasp, money belt, bank, vault

5. Look over your work on this sheet. Can you find any words that are common across your answers to the questions above? _____ *bill* _____

6. Did you figure it out? If so, what is the answer to this riddle?
   Answer: _____ *Bill* _____

For the Teacher

Riddle Title: **Short Fingers**

Halo of water, tongue of wood/Skin of stone, long I've stood./
My fingers short reach to the sky/Inside my heart men live and die.

The answer to this riddle is: <u>**Castle**</u>

This riddle has the following teachable features: Metaphor, Personification, Rhyme, and Meter.

Metaphor—expressing one thing in terms normally denoting another.

This riddle is a description of a castle that is made up of a series of quick metaphors. The first one describes the castle's moat in terms of a halo. (In this case the halo is comprised of water). The second one describes the castle's drawbridge in terms of a tongue. The third one describes the castle's wall in terms of skin. The fourth one describes the castle's crenellations in terms of fingers. The fifth metaphor describes the interior of the castle in terms of a heart. Because this is a riddle, the comparisons are implied rather than directly stated. These five metaphors effectively personify the castle (see personification section below). It is not until the listener can disentangle the metaphor that he or she can solve the riddle.

Personification—a description of something inanimate as being a living person or animal.

In this riddle the answer, castle, is an inanimate object. However it is being personified in all the following ways. It has a tongue, skin, reaching fingers, it stands, it has a heart, and it even has a halo.

Rhyme—a repetition of similar sounds in two or more words most often used in poetry and songs.

This riddle is made up of two couplets. It has the following end-of-line rhymes: wood/stood and sky/die. The rhyme scheme is *aabb*.

Meter—is the basic rhythmic structure of a verse.

The basic rhythmic structure of this verse is iambic tetrameter. That is each line is made up of four metrical feet, and the iambic foot (which is most typical of this poem) is two syllables long with an unstressed syllable followed by a stressed syllable. (da-DUM). Take a look at the stress pattern in the final couplet.

da	DUM	da	DUM	DUM	da	da	DUM
My	**fin**	gers	**short**	**reach**	to	the	**sky**
da	DUM	da	DUM	da	DUM	da	DUM
In	**side**	my	**heart**	men	**live**	and	**die**

The first line has a trochee (DUM-da) which tends to give extra emphasis to the stressed syllable in that foot. The fairly alliterative second line "skin of stone, long I've stood." comes up two syllables short, but notice that even this line retains the four stressed syllables that the underlying structure supports. The meter of this short poem can be taught as a study of acceptable variations within an overall metrical structure.

Teacher copy of student worksheet
This reference page is designed to show you what the student worksheet looks like.
Sample answers are provided in italics.

Short fingers

Halo of water, tongue of wood
Skin of stone, long I've stood.
My fingers short reach to the sky
Inside my heart men live and die.

Figuring it out!

Complete the items below:

1. This is an "I am" riddle. The speaker is an inanimate object, but it is still describing itself. What the solver needs to do is figure out who is speaking by what is being described. The riddle starts with the words "Halo of water." What can that mean? In the space below, write down everything you know about a halo.
   angels have them, they're circles, they float overhead, they are light.

2. The next thing the riddle says is tongue of wood. What can that mean? In the space below write down a list of things that can be made out of wood. HINT: your list can include big things as well as little things.
   toothpicks, houses, boats, desks, chairs, doors, tables, benches, signposts

3. The next thing the riddle says is skin of stone. What can that mean? In the space below, write down things that are made so that the outside layer is stone.
   a well, a house, a fortification, a guard tower, a castle, a stone wall

4. Putting this together, the speaker of this riddle has a watery halo, a wooden tongue, stone skin, and short fingers that reach up. It also has room enough for men to live and die in its heart. How can one thing have all these features? In the box below, draw a picture of something that has all these things.

5. Did you figure it out? If so, what is the answer to this riddle?

Answer: *Castle*

For the Teacher

Riddle Title: **Not a Kite**

Though not a kite, it needs a wind./Pull on its arm, it does not mind./Upon
large rocks it likes to sup,/But every time it throws them up.

The answer to this riddle is: **Catapult**

This riddle has the following teachable features: Homonym/Homograph, Rhyme, Personification, and Meter.

Homonym/Homograph—Homonyms In the strict linguistic sense are words that share the same spelling (homographs) and pronunciation (homophones) but that differ in meaning. However, words that have only one of these two characteristics (homographs or homophones) are often referred to as homonyms in practice.

In this riddle, the poet's use of the word "wind" is a particularly noteworthy homonym (in the sense of a homograph). For full enjoyment, this riddle is meant to be solved by the reader rather than by the listener. It is the poet's expectation that on the first time through, the reader will interpret "wind" (rhymes with sinned) as meaning air movement. After all, a kite depends upon air movement to fly. But, in fact, the meaning that actually solves the riddle is "wind" (rhymes with mind) meaning to keep proper tension on the kite string (also used to increase the potential energy of the catapult's arm before releasing a load). What actually resolves the ambiguity and nudges the reader into the correct interpretation of this word is the rhyme at the end of line two. (See the discussion of rhyme below).

Rhyme—a repetition of similar sounds in two or more words most often used in poetry and songs.

This four-line poem is made up of two rhyming couplets. It has the following end-of-line rhymes: wind/mind, sup/up. The rhyme scheme is (*aabb*). This riddle cleverly capitalizes on rhyming conventions. The rhyme in the first couplet is particularly significant because, rather than merely function to satisfy the rhyme scheme expected of the verse, this riddle uses that subliminal expectation to help the reader with the solution. The correct pronunciation of the homonym "wind" is an important clue (see the discussion Homonym/Homograph above). But it is not until the reader gets to the rhyming word (mind) at the end of line two, that it becomes apparent what the correct pronunciation (and hence meaning) ought to be.

Personification—a description of something inanimate as being a living person or animal.

In this riddle the answer, catapult, is an inanimate object. However it is being personified in the following ways. It has an arm you can pull on, but more importantly, it likes to dine (sup) on something, and it regurgitates it (throws it up). But there are also important clues in the poem to show that the object is not a person. A person usually would mind having his arm pulled. It is also the unusual person who throws up everything he eats. Finally, what person has a diet consisting of large rocks?

Meter—is the basic rhythmic structure of a verse.

This tight verse is completely constructed in iambic tetrameter with no variations. That is, each eight-syllable line is made up of four metrical feet (four iambs) where each foot starts with an unstressed syllable which is followed by a stressed syllable. (da DUM). "Though **not** a **kite**, it **needs** a **wind**" Note: The word "every" in line four is pronounced in the vernacular, and so, as a practical consequence, only has two syllable (ev/ree) rather than three (ev/er/ee).

Teacher copy of student worksheet

This reference page is designed to show you what the student worksheet looks like.

Sample answers are provided in italics.

Not a Kite

Though not a kite, it needs a wind.
Pull on its arm, it does not mind.
Upon large rocks it likes to sup,
But every time it throws them up.

Figuring it out!

This riddle is an "I saw" riddle. The thing being described by the speaker is the answer to the riddle. The job of the solver is to figure out what is actually being described.

Complete the items below:

1. The first line ends with the word wind. However, since this is a rhyming verse, we find out by looking at the end of the second line that the correct pronunciation needs to rhyme with the word mind. So we have the verb wind (like to wind up a kite string) rather than noun wind (like the moving air that keeps the kite flying). Apart from kite string, other things need to be wound. In the spaces below, first make a short list of things you can think of that need to be wound. Then describe why you think things need to be wound.

   Things that need to be wound—   alarm clock, ball of yarn, rattlesnake, fishing line
   Why things need to be wound—   so that they take up less space, winding something sometimes increases tension so it can spring.

2. The third line tells us that this thing likes to sup (eat) large rocks. Think of things that are capable of lifting up large rocks. In the space below, write down a list of things that you associate with lifting large rocks. HINT: Don't limit your list to only things that are used in the present day construction site.

   volcanoes, bulldozers, steam shovels, levers, pullys, ropes, cranes

3. The fourth line tells us that every time this things sups on large rocks, it throws them up.   In the space below, write down a list of everything you can think of that is capable of throwing large rocks up into the air.

   volcanoes, maelstroms, tornados, the circus strong man, a catapult, cannon

4. Look at what you wrote above and then read the riddle again. Did you figure it out? If so, what is the answer to this riddle?   *Catapult*

For the Teacher

Anger, cowardice and envy/ Appear to be just base emotions,/
But overhead they guide your feet/ And stipulate your forward motions.

The answer to this riddle is: **Traffic Light**

This riddle has the following teachable features: Symbolism, Rhyme, and Meter.

Symbolism—something that represents something else. It can be used to represent something invisible.

In this riddle, the poet alludes to three symbols in the first line: "Anger, cowardice, and envy." Each of these emotions is associated with a particular color; however, because this is a riddle, the poet does not provide the color for you as would be done in other kinds of poetry. Instead the reader is invited to work backwards to discover the colors red, yellow, and green respectively.

Red—Red, as a symbol, can stand for quite a number of things apart from anger. Red can also symbolize fire, the masculine, all the gods of war, the sun, vengeance, and blood lust. Anger though, as an emotion, is most closely associated with this color.

Yellow—Apart from cowardice and betrayal, the color yellow can be used to represent the sun's rays (and by extension light), faith, goodness, and intellect. Though again the emotion of cowardice is most often associated with this color.

Green—Envy, that green-eyed monster, is almost always associated with the color green. Someone can even be said to be "green with envy." Green, though, does ironic duty as it can also symbolize growth, renewal, and life. But, if one were to pick the color that represents envy, they would come up with green.

So, the associations for anger, cowardice, and envy are clearly red, yellow, and green. That is not the tricky part of the riddle. The trick is for the listener to start to associate them with the colors that they "appear" to be. Once this is done, it is not a very great leap to further associate these three particular colors with the answer, a traffic light.

Rhyme—a repetition of similar sounds in two or more words most often used in poetry and songs.

This riddle has the following end-of-line rhymes on the even lines: emotions/motions. The rhyme scheme is *abcb*.

Meter—is the basic rhythmic structure of a verse.

The basic rhythmic structure of this poem is iambic tetrameter. That is four metrical feet of two syllables with the second syllable getting the stress (da DUM) where there is an extra soft syllable at the end of lines 2 and 4 on the rhyming words. However, the first line is a variation on this basic rhythm. It is trochaic tetrameter. That is four metrical feet of two syllable with the first syllable getting the stress (DUM da).

Teacher copy of student worksheet

This reference page is designed to show you what the student worksheet looks like.
Sample answers are provided in italics.

<u>Anger</u>

Anger, cowardice and envy
Appear to be just base emotions,
But overhead they guide your feet
And stipulate your forward motions.

Figuring it out!

The answer to this riddle is a single inanimate object that is made up of three significant parts. To solve this riddle, you need to figure out what anger, cowardice, and envy represent.

Complete the items below:

1. Anger is the first emotion in this riddle. In the space below, write down a list of all the things that you associate with anger.
   Fighting, yelling, breaking things, hitting, kicking, red-faced, out of control etc...

2. Cowardice is the second emotion on the list. In the space below, write down a list of all the things that you associate with cowardice.
   Trembling, afraid, hiding, yellow-bellied, running away, retreating, avoiding a scary situation etc...

3. Envy is the third emotion listed in this riddle. In the space below, write down a list of all the things that you associate with envy.
   Wanting what someone else has, wishing you were better, green-eyed monster, hating someone lucky, good-looking, or talented etc...

4. Now, look at all the lists you have written above. Did you list any colors? What were they? If not, list the colors here that you associate most closely with these emotions.

   Anger →   <u>*Red*</u>   *Cowardice →*   <u>*Yellow*</u> *Envy →*   <u>*Green*</u>

5. Look at the list of colors you just made. What do you associate with all three of these colors?
   A traffic light

6. What is the answer to this riddle?

Answer: *Traffic Light*

For the Teacher

Riddle Title: **Starts with a Y**

Starts with a Y/ That holds a rock band/ That holds the stones/ Sent forth by hand.

The answer to this riddle is: **<u>Slingshot</u>**

This riddle has the following teachable features: Pun, Rhyme, and Meter.

Pun— is a form of word play that deliberately exploits ambiguity between similar-sounding words for humorous or rhetorical effect.

The misdirection in this brief riddle is based on a short series of puns. It begins with the powerful pun "Starts with a Y." The listener/reader is immediately led down the wrong path and assumes the answer is a word beginning with the letter Y. But the Y here actually refers to the shape of one kind of slingshot. This pun is immediately followed by another "That holds a rock band." This evokes an image of some kind of stage, concert hall, or arena because the phrase "rock band" is typically used to denote a group of musicians. The fact that this phrase could also mean "a rubber band designed to contain a rock" does not immediately occur to the native speaker of English. To extend the red herring created by these puns throughout the poem, one could imagine a concert hall that is hosting The Rolling Stones who leave the stage to thunderous applause "sent forth by hand." So, if the listener/solver is left wondering which rock venues begin with the letter Y, then the puns have done a good job of misdirection.

For class discussion—if, when discussing this poem, the conversation turns to puns, you may want to use the riddle below (where "pun" is the answer) to help introduce this topic.

Not always intended
A kick with a tee
Opening punctures
Twisting words you can't see.

Rhyme—a repetition of similar sounds in two or more words most often used in poetry and songs.

This riddle has the following end-of-line rhymes on the even lines: band/hand. The rhyme scheme is *abcb*.

Meter—is the basic rhythmic structure of a verse.

This is a very short poem. It is so short, in fact, that each of the last two lines can be considered to be a single metrical foot, a tetrasyllable, called a diamb. (da DUM da DUM). The diamb then might be considered to be the basic rhythmic building block of this poem, but the poem is too short and irregular for this claim to be particularly strong. The poem may be more useful to talk about in its variations on rhythmical structure rather than its adherence to an underlying rhythmical idea. The first line then is made up of two disyllables (a trochee—DUM da—and an iamb—da DUM). The second line though starts with an iamb, but this is followed by a trisyllable (an anapest—da da DUM). The two diambs finish the poem. The poet could have easily conformed more to a diambic structure, (for example, the first line could have read "It starts with Y"—da DUM da DUM), but this choice takes the meaning too far in the wrong direction of the pun. The regular rhythm then, gives way to competing considerations of the riddle.

Teacher copy of student worksheet

This reference page is designed to show you what the student worksheet looks like.

Sample answers are provided in italics.

Starts with a Y

Starts with a Y
That holds a rock band
That holds the stones
Sent forth by hand.

Figuring it out!

Complete the items below:

1. The first line of this riddle says "Starts with a Y." But "Y" here is not the letter of the alphabet. It is actually a shape. Think of things that have this shape. In the space below, write down things you can think of that are shaped like the letter Y.
   tree branch, propeller, peace sign, fork in the road, witching rod

2. The second line of this riddle says "That holds a rock band." In this case, though, the "rock band" is not the kind that you would see at a rock concert. What else could these words mean? In the space below write down a list of possible meanings for the words rock band.
   necklace with beads or precious stones, a group of rocks, pouch of pebbles

3. The third line of this riddle says "That holds the stones." Think of things that can do the job of holding stones. In the space below, write down a list of things that could be used to hold stones.
   a string, a pouch, a jar, a purse, a hand, a necklace, a bowl, a pond

4. The last line says "Sent forth by hand." The hand in this line is sending forth the stones from the line above. Think about what this could mean. In the space below, write down a list of your ideas about what it could mean to send forth "stones" by hand.
   This could mean throwing stones in some way or pressing a trigger

5. Look at what you have written above. The answer to this riddle is some kind of contraption that looks like a Y that is attached to a band that sends forth stones.

   Did you figure it out? If so, what is the answer to this riddle?
   Answer: _____*Slingshot*_____

For the Teacher

Riddle Title: **Five Points**

I once was a great mausoleum,/But, cursed, I became a museum./And betwixt my points, five,/
Some were buried alive./Now others line up just to see 'em.

The answer to this riddle is: **<u>Pyramid</u>**

This riddle has the following teachable features: Rhyme, Meter and Limerick

Rhyme—a repetition of similar sounds in two or more words most often used in poetry and songs.

This riddle has the following end-of-line rhymes: mausoleum/museum/to see 'em and also five/alive.
This riddle follows the form of a limerick so its rhyme scheme is (*aabba*)

Meter—is the basic rhythmic structure of a verse.

Since this is a limerick, this riddle's basic structure is made up of feet with three beats. Some describe the limerick as mostly based on an anapest meter (da-da-DUM) but others believe that the basic structure can best be described in terms of an amphibrachic meter (da-DUM-da). Often you will find minor variations to the basic rhythmic formula. For this riddle, then, the first, second and fifth lines are each made up of three amphibrachic feet.

Foot 1			Foot 2			Foot 3		
da	DUM	da	da	DUM	da	da	DUM	da
I	**once**	was	a	**great**	maus-	o-	**le-**	um
But	**cursed**	I	be	**came**	a	mu-	**se-**	um
Now	**oth-**	ers	line	**up**	just	to	**see**	'em

The third and fourth lines in a limerick have only two feet which are anapestic (da-da-DUM/da-da-DUM).

And be — **twixt** my points **five**
Some were **bur** — ied al — **ive**

Limerick—is a verse form that is exactly five lines in length and adheres to a strict rhyme scheme (see above). The meter, as discussed above, is usually a mixture of anapestic or amphibrachic feet often with some minor variation. Limericks are written mainly to be witty or humorous, often with ribald humor. They may have developed in Ireland among the Maigue Poets.

Witty and humorous limericks are not always ribald

A canner exceedingly canny
One morning remarked to his granny
A canner can can
Anything that he can
But a canner can't can a can, can he?

This poetic warning is ironically comical:

The limerick packs laughs anatomical
In space that is quite economical,
But the good ones I've seen
So seldom are clean,
And the clean ones so seldom are comical.

Extra Activity: Have your students see if they can write a poem in limerick form.

Teacher copy of student worksheet

This reference page is designed to show you what the student worksheet looks like.

Sample answers are provided in italics.

Five Points

I once was a great mausoleum,
But, cursed, I became a museum.
And betwixt my points, five,
Some were buried alive.
Now others line up just to see 'em.

Figuring it out!

The speaker of this riddle is an inanimate object, but it is describing itself. This is an example of an "I am" type of riddle. In order to solve this type of riddle, one needs to figure out what is being self-described by the speaker.

Complete the items below:

1. The first line uses the word "mausoleum." A mausoleum can be described as a type of tomb, perhaps a monument to honor the dead who are laid to rest there. In the space below make a list of any of the famous mausoleums or tombs of which you are aware. If you like, you can begin your list with "Grant's tomb."

   Grant's tomb, Taj Mahal, Lenin's mausoleum, Abraham Linclon's tomb, Miles mausoleum, royal mausoleum, the pyramids of Egypt

2. In line two, this mausoleum claims to have been "cursed." The kind of curse being discussed here is a wish that something bad will happen to someone else. If the wish is against you, then you are cursed. Think about all the curses you may have heard about. In the space below write down as many of these as you can remember. If you like, you may start your list with "A witch's curse."

   A witch's curse, the curse of the mummy, the curse of Eve, the unforgivable curses, the imperious curse, the cruciatus curse

3. The mausoleum that is "speaking" this riddle claims that some were buried alive "…betwixt my points, five." The word "betwixt" basically means the same thing as "between." So, this means that some were buried alive between the mausoleum's five points. A triangle has three points. In the space below write down a list of geometric shapes. Hint—don't limit yourself to two dimensional shapes.

   Circle, triangle, rectangle, pentagon, square, octogaon, dodeca-hedron sphere, pyramid, cube, prism, cylinder septagon, polygon, decagon

   Look at the list you just wrote. Do any of these shapes have exactly five points?

4. Did you figure out what this mausoleum is?

   If so, what is the answer to this riddle?   *Pyramid*

For the Teacher

Riddle Title: **Five Lines**

> A plate upon which no one dines/ In a diamond that never shines./
> A place to store/More plans for war,/ Described by just five lines.

The answer to this riddle is: **<u>Pentagon</u>**

This riddle has the following teachable features: Rhyme, Homonym and Limerick.

Rhyme—a repetition of similar sounds in two or more words most often used in poetry and songs.

This riddle has the following end-of-line rhymes: dines/shines/lines and also store/war. This riddle follows the rhyme scheme of a limerick which is (*aabba*).

Homonym—words that share the same spelling (homographs) and pronunciation (homophones) but that differ in meaning.

In this riddle, the poet's deliberate use of four homonyms is noteworthy. The four homonyms are 'plate,' 'diamond,' 'described,' and 'lines.' In the first line, it is as if the poet is saying that the answer to the riddle is a plate, however it is not the one you are probably thinking of because nobody eats off this plate. In the second line the poet implies that this plate is in a diamond, but not the one you are thinking of because this one never shines. In fact the plate is a reference to home 'plate' in a baseball 'diamond,' but the homonyms are both strong enough to befuddle the hearer. The final homonyms "described" and "lines" are interesting because the poet is using two different meanings of these words simultaneously. In one sense, the answer of the riddle can be described in short order by just the five lines of text that make up this riddle. But also the shape of a pentagon is actually "described" by being drawn with exactly five lines. This is an extremely artful pun because it works so well given either of these two meanings of these two homonyms.

Limerick—is a verse form that is exactly five lines in length and adheres to a strict rhyme scheme (see above). This riddle is *not* a limerick, but it is close. The previous riddle in this book, "Five Points" *is* a limerick. Studying the difference between these two poems may be instructive to students who are new to the concept of a limerick. Both poems are five lines long. Both have the exact same rhyme scheme (*aabba*). Lines 1, 2, and 5 in both riddles are relatively long, while lines 3 and 4 are short. All this is true of the requirements of a limerick. The significant difference between the two riddles, though, is the meter. A pure limerick may be said to be made up of three amphibrachic feet (short-long-short) in lines 1, 2, and 5; and also two anapestic feet (short-short-long) in lines 3 and 4. The beat of a pure limerick, then, would sound like this:

```
da-DUM-da  da-DUM-da  da-DUM-da
da-DUM-da  da-DUM-da  da-DUM-da
da-da-DUM  da-da-DUM
da-da-DUM  da-da-DUM
da-DUM-da  da-DUM-da  da-DUM-da
```

Though there are often minor variations to this theme in poems that all agree are still limericks, the meter of *this* poem is just too far off for it to be considered a limerick. *Hearing* the differences in meter between these two poems ("Five Points" and "Five Lines") will help increase student appreciation of the limerick verse form.

Extra Activity: Have your students see if they can write a poem in limerick form.

Teacher copy of student worksheet

This reference page is designed to show you what the student worksheet looks like.

Sample answers are provided in italics.

Five Lines

A plate upon which no one dines
In a diamond that never shines.
A place to store
More plans for war,
Described by just five lines.

Figuring it out!

The answer to this riddle is a single word, but there are three different major clues in the poem that will help you figure out the answer.

Complete the items below:

1. The first major clue is in the first two lines. The key words are "plate" and "diamond." The plate is not the kind that is used to serve food, and the diamond is not the shiny kind. In the spaces below, first write a list of all the different types of plates you can think of, and then write a list of everything you can associate with the word "diamond."

    Plate—china, tectonic plate, plate glass, home plate
    Diamond—diamondback rattlesnake, diamond mine, baseball diamond

2. The second major clue is in lines 3 and 4. "A place to store more plans for war." What could that mean? Where does one store war plans? In the space below write down some of the things you know about planning for war.

    you need an army, you need generals, you need maps and watches, you need to know where the other army is. you need a tent

3. The third major clue is in line five. "Described by just five lines." While it is true that this riddle is five lines long, and that those lines are a description of sorts, this is not the only meaning of these words. Another kind of line is a straight line that you can draw. In the box below, draw a picture of something, but only use five lines to do it.

4. Look at what you drew.

    Can you describe what you drew in one word? _______*Pentagon*_______

5. Did you figure it out?

    If so, what is the answer to this riddle? _______*Pentagon*_______

For the Teacher

Riddle Title: **Riddle Me This**

Riddle me this. Answer me try./Brother of who, when, where, and why./
What is my name?/What can I be?/I told you! Now you tell me!

The answer to this riddle is: <u>**What**</u>

This riddle has the following teachable features: Alliteration, Personification, and Rhyme.

Alliteration—repetition of the same consonant sound at the beginning of several words in succession.

In this poem, the phrase "...who, when, where, and why" can be used to illustrate the poet's use of alliteration.

Personification—a description of something inanimate as being a living person or animal.

In this riddle, who, when, where, and why are described as "brothers" to each other and to the speaker of the riddle (what).   To make these words into brothers shows the poet's use of personification.

Rhyme—a repetition of similar sounds in two or more words most often used in poetry and songs.

This riddle has the following end-of-line rhyming couplets: try/why and be/me. The rhyme scheme is *abbcdd*.

Unique features—This riddle contains two traditional riddle devices.

In the history of riddles there is sometimes a cue line at the beginning that lets the listener know that what follows is actually a riddle. The phrase "Riddle me this" is one such line that is not uncommon to riddling in general. It is followed by "Answer me try" which is also meant to cue the reader/listener that it is time to put on a thinking cap. Other riddle openers include: "Me riddle me ree/Not a man shall explain this riddle on to me" which is more of a challenge than a mere warning; and "Come a riddle come a riddle/Come a rat trat trat." These kinds of openings are often used also to set up a following rhyme.

The last line of this riddle "I told you! Now you tell me!" is also not entirely unknown in the riddling tradition. This kind of line can be used to point out a homophone. As in the riddle:

What's up in the sky?
Knot on a tree?
I told you, now you tell me!

The answer to the above is a "knot on a tree." In the oral tradition, the listener would hear "not on a tree" and would need the last line to point out the need to go back and discover that the key word was not "not" but instead "knot" and thereby discover the answer. In *Riddle Me This* the poet writes "What is my name." The listener needs to go back and discover my name is "What."

Teacher copy of student worksheet
This reference page is designed to show you what the student worksheet looks like.
Sample answers are provided in italics.

Riddle Me This

Riddle me this.
Answer me try.
Brother of who, when, where, and why.
What is my name?
What can I be?
I told you! Now you tell me!

Figuring it out!

Complete the items below:

1. In this riddle, the speaker claims to be the brother of *who*, *when*, *where*, and *why*. Brothers often share some kind of family resemblance. How do these four words, these "brothers," resemble each other? In the space below, write down any similarities you notice between the words **who**, **when**, **where** and **why**:
   Each is one syllable long. They are questions. Start with "wh"

2. Who? When? Where? Why? These are examples of question words sometimes called WH words. Often they are grouped together with "How?" Newspaper reporters are trained to answer these questions in their articles when writing a story. In the lines below, write down as many WH question words as you can think of:
   Who? When? Where? Why? What? Which? Whoever?

3. Look at the list you just wrote. Are there any words on that list that are not Who? When? Where? or Why? If so, write just those words in the space below.
   What? Which? Whoever?

4. A good hint for this riddle is "What is the answer to this riddle." Notice that this hint does *not* have question mark even though it sounds like a question. If this hint is not a question, then what else can the hint mean? In the space below, rephrase the hint but be careful not to turn it into a question:
   The answer to this riddle is what.

5. Did you figure it out? If so, what is the answer to this riddle? *What*

For the Teacher

Riddle Title: **Upon My Perch**

Relaxed I sit upon my perch,/'Til suddenly I give a lurch./And off I speed on wing-tips three/Before my prey can think to flee./I make its flesh and tendons part/And claw my way into its heart.

The answer to this riddle is: **Arrow**

This riddle has the following teachable features: Metaphor, Personification, Rhyme, and Meter.

Metaphor—expressing one thing in terms normally denoting another.

This riddle is an example of an implicit somewhat extended metaphor. Rather than explicitly stating that an arrow is a bird of prey (and thus revealing the answer) the poet shows the many ways that one could think of an arrow as having the same attributes as a bird of prey. After all, it sits on a perch, flies with speed, and has wingtips. It also claws at its prey in a deadly way. The implicit metaphor is a well-established riddle form. Humpty Dumpty is one familiar example.

Personification—a description of something inanimate as being a living person or animal.

In this riddle the answer, "arrow," is an inanimate object. However it is being personified in all the following ways. It sits relaxed. It has prey. It claws its way as if it has intent. All of these show the poet's use of personification.

Rhyme—a repetition of similar sounds in two or more words most often used in poetry and songs.

This riddle has the following end-of-line rhyming couplets: perch/lurch; three/flee; and part/heart. The rhyme scheme is *aabbcc*.

Meter—is the basic rhythmic structure of a verse.

This riddle is an example of iambic tetrameter with no variation. Each line has four metrical feet, and each foot is an iamb with the stress on the second syllable. One way to express this is:

da DUM da DUM da DUM da DUM

For an informative additional exercise, have your students clap this stress pattern with alternating soft and loud claps as the poem is read aloud.

Relaxed I sit upon my perch,
'Til suddenly I give a lurch.
And off I speed on wing-tips three
Before my prey can think to flee.
I make its flesh and tendons part
And claw my way into its heart.

Teacher copy of student worksheet

This reference page is designed to show you what the student worksheet looks like.

Sample answers are provided in italics.

<u>Upon My Perch</u>

Relaxed I sit upon my perch,
'Til suddenly I give a lurch.
And off I speed on wing-tips three
Before my prey can think to flee.
I make its flesh and tendons part
And claw my way into its heart.

Figuring it out!

Complete the items below:

1. In this riddle, the speaker claims to have three wingtips. Wingtips sometimes have feathers. Birds have two wingtips. There are no birds with three wingtips. The speaker of the riddle cannot be a bird even though it has a perch and claw. In the space below, write down anything you can think of that has three wingtips.
rockets, missiles, planes, helicopters, paper airplanes, darts,
engine propellers, triangles, t-formation, theatrical stage

2. Birds of prey do attack small animals and do damage to them with their claws. However, since the answer to the riddle is not a bird, but still it attacks its prey very swiftly and penetrates even to the heart, it is a deadly opponent. Think of things that are not birds, but can still be very fast and deadly. Write a list of these things in the space below.
rattlesnakes, cobras, bullets, spears, swords, arrows, missiles,
rockets, harpoons, crossbow bolts, eggplants, knives, daggers

3. Look at the list you just wrote. Are all items on your list living things? What if the answer to the riddle is not a living thing? Can you think of non-living fast and deadly things? If so, write a short list of these things in the space below.
bullets, spears, swords, arrows, missiles

4. Are there any things on the lists you wrote above that fly through the air? The speaker of the riddle sits on a perch, then speeds towards its prey using three wingtips. What non-living, deadly things fly through the air using three feathers?
Arrows

5. Did you figure it out? If so, what is the answer to this riddle?
Arrow

For the Teacher

Riddle Title: **Inside a Pod**

> One that rests inside a pod/The one of us not I/Place the ball before you shoot/
> A drink that's sometimes high/Not who or what, where, when or how/A bee could name me now.

The answer to this riddle is: **Putty**

This riddle has the following teachable features: Alliteration, Homophone, Rhyme, Ballad Stanza and Charade

Alliteration—repetition of the same consonant sound at the beginning of several words in succession.

In this poem, the line "Not who or what, where, when or how" can be used to illustrate the poet's use of alliteration.

Homonym/Homophone—Homonyms In the strict linguistic sense are words that share the same spelling (homographs) and pronunciation (homophones) but that differ in meaning. However, words that have only one of these two characteristics (homographs or homophones) are often referred to as homonyms in practice.

In this riddle, the poet uses a series of five homonyms of the homophone variety. If you answer correctly any of the first five questions, you will have produced a homophone for a letter of the alphabet. (They are pea, you, tee, tea, and why.) Put them all together, and you spell putty.

Rhyme—a repetition of similar sounds in two or more words most often used in poetry and songs.

This poem consists of a quatrain (see the section on the Ballad Stanza below) followed by a couplet. The end-of-line rhyming words are I/high and how/now.

The rhyme scheme is (*abcb ee*).

Ballad Stanza—is the four-line stanza, known as a quatrain, most often found in the folk ballad. This form consists of alternating four- and three-stress lines. Usually only the second and fourth lines rhyme (in an abcb pattern).

The first four lines of this riddle are in ballad stanza form with alternating seven and six syllable lines. The longer are four-stress lines, and the shorter are three-stress lines. The bold syllables reproduced below show the stress pattern.

> **One** that **rests** in — **side** a **pod**/The **one** of **us** not **I**/
> **Place** the **ball** be — **fore** you **shoot**/A **snack** that's **some** — times **high**

Charade—a literary exercise playing on letters or syllables.

This riddle is a type of charade that plays on letters. The answer to each of the first five lines is a letter which the spelling bee of the last line could put together as P-U-T-T-Y.

Unique Feature—a charade is an unusual type of riddle. "Inside a Pod" plays on letters. The riddle below plays with syllables. Try this one with your students to further illustrate the charade.

> I'm a bird/That you can name/Beginning with/A kind of game./
> If next I play/I'm never out/It's me or nothing/To end the bout.

Answer: Cardinal (card-in-all)

Teacher copy of student worksheet

This reference page is designed to show you what the student worksheet looks like.

Sample answers are provided in italics.

Inside a Pod

One that rests inside a pod
The one of us not I
Place the ball before you shoot

A drink that's sometimes high
Not who or what, where, when or how
A bee could name me now

Figuring it out!

This is an unusual riddle because it is really a combination of many small riddles. In order to solve it, you will need to solve a number of small riddles and then put those answers together to solve the whole riddle. The answer you are looking for is a single word.

Complete the items below:

1. The first clue is "one who rests inside a pod." In the space below, write down anything you can associate with the word "pod."

   peas, print-on-demand, podcast, the pod hotel, the ipod

2. The second clue is "The one of us not I." If there are two of us, which is the one of us that is not I?

   You

3. The third clue is "place the ball before you shoot." Think of all the games you can where you need to do this. Make a list of the places where you need to place a ball.

   The corner, over the plate, on a tee for teeball, the cueball

4. The fourth clue is "A drink that is sometimes high." Can you think of any drinks where people use the word "high" to name them? List any you can think of in the space below.

   Hi-C, high tea, high-school cafeteria lunch

5. The fifth clue is "Not who or what, where, when or how." What question words are missing from this list? Write them in the space below.

   Which? Why? Wherefore?

6. The last line says that "A bee can name me now." But this bee is not an insect that flies around to collect pollen. How many other kinds of bees are there? Write down as many as you can think of in the space below.

   a sewing bee, the letter bee, a spelling bee, beeswax

7. Now, look at all the answers you gave for 1 through 5 above. Are there any similar kinds of answers? Do any of the answers you gave sound like the names of letters of the alphabet? If so, write those words here.

   pea, you, tee, tea, why

8. Did you figure it out? If so, what is the answer to this riddle? *Putty*

For the Teacher

Riddle Title: **Dormitory**

It's clear a dormitory/Is indeed a dirty room/And that a schoolmaster/Matches the classroom./But did you know a funeral/Is a form of real fun?/And that eleven plus two/Is the same as twelve plus one?

The answer to this riddle is: **Anagram**

Special Note: The word *anagram* means a rearrangement of the letters of a word or phrase that produces a new word or phrase using all the original letters exactly once. Your students may be unfamiliar with this word, but, through the worksheet, they might discover this device used in the riddle. This riddle can be used to teach the word anagram and this concept.

This riddle has the following teachable features: Irony, Rhyme, and Synonym.

Irony—is a situation in which there is an incongruity, discordance, or unintended connection with truth, which goes strikingly beyond the most simple and evident meaning of words or actions.

In this riddle, the idea that a funeral is real fun is intentionally ironic. The poet's use of this obvious untruth on the literal level is a clue that can lead to the "true" answer in the mathematical sense. Notice that this use of irony falls between other clues that actually make sense on the literal level. For example, it is not hard to conceive of a dormitory as being a dirty room. This use of irony for the sake of mere word play can serve as an introduction to the broader use of irony in literature.

Rhyme—a repetition of similar sounds in two or more words most often used in poetry and songs.

This riddle has the following end-of-line rhymes on the even lines classroom/room and fun/one. The rhyme scheme is *abcb defe*.

Synonym—synonyms are different words with identical or very similar meanings.

This riddle functions on the surface as a way of pointing out the similarities between two concepts. "dormitory" is synonymous with "dirty room." The "schoolmaster" is likened to the "classroom" and the mathematical similarity between the terms 12 + 1 and 11+2 (both equal to 13) is, on the surface, obvious. The fact that "funeral" is in no way synonymous with "real fun" gives the solver the chance to see that more is going on here than the literal interpretation.

Unique Features: This riddle is all about anagrams.

Anagrams can be clever word-play devices that can be used to show similarities (or differences) between the anagram subject and object. One famous example is:

William Shakespeare = I am a weakish speller

This anagram has an added humorous dimension considering the spelling of the word "weakish." For an amusing additional exercise, have your students write out their first and last name, and then see if they can anagram those letters into another word or phrase.

Teacher copy of student worksheet

This reference page is designed to show you what the student worksheet looks like.

Sample answers are provided in italics.

Dormitory

It's clear a dormitory
Is indeed a dirty room
And that a schoolmaster
Matches the classroom.
But did you know a funeral
Is a form of real fun?
And that eleven plus two
Is the same as twelve plus one?

Figuring it out!

Complete the items below:

This riddle is made up of four clues. Each clue is two lines long. The third clue does not seem to make much logical sense. Not many people think that having a funeral is fun, and yet the riddle tells us that "...a funeral is a form of real fun". Since an actual funeral is not fun, let's instead, turn this into an equation. The equation for clue #3 is:

(Clue #3) Funeral = Real fun

Help make the equations for the other three clues by filling out the blank spaces below:

(Clue #1) Dormitory   =   *dirty room*

(Clue #2) Schoolmaster =   *the classroom*

Clue #4) Eleven plus two =   *twelve plus one*

Look at what you just did. Did you write the numerals "12 + 1," or did you write out the words "twelve plus one"? Since the riddle uses the words, you should too. In the space below, write down any similarities you see between the words on the left side of each equation and the words on the right hand side. (Hint: How many times does the letter "w" appear?)

The letter "w" appears once on the left (in the word "two") and once on the right (in the word "twelve"). There is the same number of letters on the left side as the right side of each equation, and the same letters appear on each side of each equation, but in a different order.

Did you figure it out? If so, describe what you notice about each of the four clues, or if you know it, write the one-word answer to the riddle?

Answer: *Anagram*

For the Teacher

Riddle Title: **The Hunter**

The hunter far and wide will roam,/Like a ghost of sun and shadow./First she'll brush then find the comb,/And then put on a dancing show./Mother waits inside her home,/Where golden treasure flows.

The answer to this riddle is: <u>**Bee**</u>

This riddle has the following teachable features: Alliteration, Consonance, Simile, Pun, Rhyme, and Near Rhyme or Half Rhyme.

Alliteration—repetition of the same consonant sound at the beginning of several words in succession.

In line 1 of this riddle, the words "...wide will roam" is an example of alliteration.

Consonance—repetition of the same consonant sound within a phrase.

Consider the "s" sound this portion of line two. "...ghost of sun and shadow."

Simile—a figure of speech comparing two unlike things using either the word "like" or "as."

In this riddle, the unnamed "bee" is being compared implicitly to a ghost who has an attribute of sun and an attribute of shadow. The solver is left to question how this thing could be "<u>**Like**</u> a ghost of sun and shadow." One aspect of sun is that it is yellow while shadow is black. Using this aspect, then, the object is both yellow and black.

Pun— is a form of word play that deliberately exploits ambiguity between similar-sounding words for humorous or rhetorical effect.

In this riddle the poet deliberately uses both the words "brush" and "comb" in an attempt to misdirect the solver. At first glance the middle two lines evoke an image of a woman primping before performing a dance; when, in fact, the "brush" refers to the bee brushing parts of a flower to get pollen, and then finding the honey "comb."

Rhyme—a repetition of similar sounds in two or more words most often used in poetry and songs. And

Near Rhyme or Half Rhyme—a partial or imperfect rhyme often using only assonance or consonace.

This riddle has both true rhymes and near rhymes. If we consider the rhyme scheme to be *ababab*, we will find that the rhyming words roam/comb/home are examples of true rhyme. The other rhyming words, shadow/show/flows, are not true rhymes, but they are similar enough to be considered near rhymes. This is a good example riddle for introducing the differences between true rhymes and near rhymes.

Teacher copy of student worksheet

This reference page is designed to show you what the student worksheet looks like.

Sample answers are provided in italics.

The Hunter

The hunter far and wide will roam,
Like a ghost of sun and shadow.
First she'll brush then find the comb,
And then put on a dancing show.
Mother waits inside her home,
Where golden treasure flows.

Figuring it out!

Complete the items below:

1. In this riddle, the hunter is like "a ghost of sun and shadow." To help figure out what the hunter is like, we should consider what the sun is like and what a shadow is like. In the spaces below, write down things that you associate with "sun" and "shadow."

   Sun— warm, hot, bright, burning, yellow, lotion, beach, summer, center of the solar system, flares, stars, far away, sunset
   Shadow— dark, cold, evil, hiding, "The Shadow knows," black, night, clouds, shade trees, image, hard to see, secrecy, spies

2. The third line mentions a "comb" and a "brush." But these words have nothing to do with styling hair. In the spaces below write down as many meanings of these words as you can.

   Brush— toothbrush, toilet brush, dog brush, brush off somebody,
   Comb—— fine tooth comb, rooster comb, honeycomb, comb the beach, comb the search area, comb over, lash comb

3. In the last two lines, the mother is waiting in a special home. This is a home where "golden treasure" flows. Who lives in a home with golden treasure? Why does it flow? Water flows, but gold coins do not. In the lines below write down other things that flow.

   milk, oil, vinegar, rivers, streams, liquids

   Look at the list you just wrote. Are any of these things "golden" in color?

4. Putting it all together. From the sun and shadow clues did you write down their colors? What are they? What else has these colors? What is it with these colors that needs to find a comb (different from a hair comb)? Who is the female who waits in this "hunter's" home among the flowing golden treasure? You may use the lines below to help you gather your thoughts.

   Colors of sun and shadow? *yellow, black* Kind of comb? *honey* Who waits at home? *queen*

5. Did you figure out who the hunter is? If so, what is the answer to this riddle?   *Bee*

For the Teacher

Riddle Title: **The Ballet**

> I start off the ballet./I'm a dance. I'm a room./I can also be found in/A circus balloon./
> If you're having fun,/You might have one of me./Hard, soft and basket;/Foot, base and tee.

The answer to this riddle is: **Ball**

This riddle has the following teachable features: Compound Words and Rhyme,

Compound Words—are made when two words are joined to form a new word.

In this riddle there are seven examples of incomplete compound words. They are room, hard, soft, basket, foot, base, and tee. One traditional logic puzzle provides a list of clue words such as this. The solver is expected to provide the other part of the compound word that fits all cases. In this case, the word "ball" fits the bill. Thus the compounds ballroom, hardball, softball, basketball, football, baseball, and tee-ball will result if the correct answer is applied.

For an amusing additional exercise, have your students write down a list of compound words from their own experience where one of the parts of the compound is common to all words. (e.g., "bluebird", "bluejay" and "bluebell.") Then they should rewrite their list but remove the common word (i.e., bird, jay, & bell). Now she can exchange her list with another student to see if he can figure out one word that will successfully turn her list into compound words.

Rhyme—a repetition of similar sounds in two or more words most often used in poetry and songs.

This riddle has the following end-of-line rhymes on the even lines. Room/balloon, me/tee. The rhyme scheme is *abcb defe*.

Unique features— This riddle contains three distinct types of clues. In addition to the list of compound words (CLUE TYPE 3 on the student worksheet) discussed above, there are these two additional types of clues.

CLUE TYPE 1 –Is where the answer "ball" is given as part of the larger words **BALL**et and **BALL**oon. Consider the following riddle:

> The beginning of eternity
> The end of time and space
> The beginning of every end
> And the end of every place.

This kind of riddle contains the answer within the lines of the riddle. In the riddle above the correct answer is the letter "e."

CLUE TYPE 2—is where the intended answer "ball" is a specific example of a general case. The key words here are "dance" and "having fun." If you go to a dance with Cinderella you might go to a "ball." And if you have fun there, you might come home and tell people you had a "ball."

Teacher copy of student worksheet
This reference page is designed to show you what the student worksheet looks like.
Sample answers are provided in italics.

<u>The Ballet</u>

I start off the ballet.
I'm a dance. I'm a room.
I can also be found in
A circus balloon.
If you're having fun,
You might have one of me.
Hard, soft and basket;
Foot, base and tee.

Figuring it out!

Complete the items below:

1. In this riddle, the speaker claims to be associated with many things. Of the four clues in the first four lines (ballet, dance, room, and circus balloon) two of them (ballet and circus balloon) are what we will call CLUE TYPE 1. In the spaces below write these two clues.

CLUE TYPE 1 _____ *ballet* _____ *circus balloon* _____

 Look at what you just wrote. Do you notice any similarities between these two clues?

2. "Dance" is an example of a different kind of clue. Call this CLUE TYPE 2. In the space below write down the names of different kinds of dances..

CLUE TYPE 2— DANCE *break dancing, contra, folk, waltz, fox trot, square dancing, ballet, modern, line dancing, step dancing*

3. In the second half of this riddle, there is a CLUE TYPE 2 (having fun). Another way to say having fun is to say "I'm having a good time." or "I'm having a blast." In the space below, write down different ways of saying "having fun."

CLUE TYPE 2—HAVING FUN *kickin' it, getting down, celebrating, partying, having a ball, partying hearty, joining in, letting loose*

4. The riddle also contains seven examples of CLUE TYPE 3. The words room, hard, soft, basket, foot, base, and tee are all parts of different compound words. If you join the word "school" to the word "house" you get the compound word "schoolhouse." The CLUE TYPE 3 words are each one part of a compound word. The other part of the compound is the same across all seven clue words. It can go either before or after the clue words (example: foot____). In the spaces below write as many compound words as you can think of using these seven clues.

CLUE TYPE 3--COMPOUNDS *footloose, foothold, football, basket case, Easter basket, basketball, hardball, softball, baseball*

Did you figure it out? If so, what is the answer to this riddle? _____ *Ball* _____

For the Teacher

Riddle Title: **A Dozen Royals**

A dozen Royals gathered round,/Entertained by two who clowned./Each King there had servants ten,/Though none of them were also men./The lowest servant sometimes might,/Defeat the King in a fair fight./A weapon stout, a priceless jewel,/The beat of life, a farmer's tool.

The answer to this riddle is: **<u>Deck of Cards</u>**

This riddle has the following teachable features: Alliteration, Consonance, Metaphor, Personification, Rhyme, and Meter.

Alliteration—repetition of the same consonant sound at the beginning of several words in succession. In line six of this poem, the phrase "...fair fight" is an example of alliteration.

Consonance—repetition of the same consonant sound within a phrase. Consider the "s" sound in line five. "The lowest servant sometimes might"

Metaphor—expressing one thing in terms normally denoting another.

There are four quick metaphors in the final couplet of this poem, each having to do with one of the four suits in a deck of cards. That is, a weapon stout = a club, a priceless jewel = a diamond, the beat of life = a heart, and a farmer's tool = a spade. The named suits are really only distinguishing marks on a deck of cards. The poet is alluding to each undeclared suit metaphorically as a series of four related but distinct clues for the listener.

Personification—a description of something inanimate as being a living person.

The cards in a deck are inanimate, however, in this riddle the royal cards are "entertained" by the jokers. The numbered cards of the same suit all "serve" that royal family. Sometimes the king and the ace actually fight. All these are examples of personification. In line four (though none of them were also men) the poet tips his hand somewhat by revealing that perhaps these servants are not actually people, although an easy misinterpretation would be that they are either women or children. In a way, the poet is here pointing out that he is simply employing personification. This functions to help the solver get on the right track.

Rhyme—a repetition of similar sounds in two or more words most often used in poetry and songs.

This eight-line poem is made up of four rhyming couplets. It has the following end-of-line rhymes: round/clowned, ten/men, might/fight, and jewel/tool. The rhyme scheme is (*aa bb cc dd*).

Meter—is the basic rhythmic structure of a verse.

The rhythmic structure of this verse is iambic tetrameter.. That is, the typical line is eight syllables long and is made up of four metrical feet (four iambs). Each iamb starts with an unstressed syllable which is followed by a stressed syllable. (da DUM). The first line is a good example of this basic rhythmic pattern:

da	**DUM**	da	**DUM**	da	**DUM**	da	**DUM**
A	**doz**	en	**Roy**	als	**gath**	ered	**round**

Minor variances from this structure are in lines two and three where each has only seven syllables. It is easiest to explain this variance by having your students think of these lines as missing the initial unstressed syllable. Both of these lines begin with a stressed syllable which is followed by three iambs. Note: The diphthong "jewel" in line seven can be thought of as a one syllable word like "tool" in line eight. Each really has two vowel sounds in rapid succession.

A Dozen Royals

A dozen Royals gathered round,
Entertained by two who clowned.
Each King there had servants ten,
Though none of them were also men.

The lowest servant sometimes might,
Defeat the King in a fair fight.
A weapon stout, a priceless jewel,
The beat of life, a farmer's tool.

Figuring it out!

This riddle is a description of several aspects of the same thing. This thing has several components, but the answer to the riddle is really only one thing that names the entire collection.

Complete the items below:

To get a general idea of how many things are in this collection, study the poem to find some numbers. Answer each of the following questions with a number:

1. How many "Royals" are there? *12*

2. How many clowns are there? *2*

3. How many servants does each king have? *10*

4. The riddle does not say how many of these royals actually are kings, but at least some of them are. Answer this yes/no question. According to the riddle, is there more than one king? *yes*

5. Assume that the clowns are not also servants or royals. If so, then at a minimum, there are **at least** how many things total in this collection? *at least 34*

Questions 6 – 9 are based on the list found in the last two lines of the riddle.

6. Make a list of all the stout, handheld weapons you can think of.
mace, billy club, nightstick, cugle, warhammer, two-handed sword

7. Make a list of all the valuable jewels you can think of.
diamonds, rubies, emeralds, sapphires, opals, amethysts

8. What is the beat of life? List your ideas about what this phrase might mean.
music, rock & roll, heartbeat, falling in love, seasons, day & night

9. List as many farmers' tools as you can think of.
hoe, shovel, tractor, plow, axe, milk pail, stool, reaper, scythe, harness

10. Look for relationships between things on your lists above. Did you figure it out? If so, what is the answer to this riddle?

Answer: *Deck of Cards*

For the Teacher

Riddle Title: **The Prisoner**

> A prisoner he might appear,/Not gagged but strongly bound./Forced to tell his tale again,/He
> does and makes no sound./His questioner just sits and stares/And nothing's ever heard./
> He's then released because, in truth,/He's told them every word.

The answer to this riddle is: **Book**

This riddle has the following teachable features: Metaphor, Personification, Pun, Rhyme, and Meter.

Metaphor—expressing one thing in terms normally denoting another.

This riddle is an example of an implicit metaphor. It does not explicitly state that a book is a bound captive (and thus revealing the answer). Rather, the poet shows the many ways that one could think of a book, as having the same attributes as a human prisoner without ever mentioning the book. It is "strongly bound" and "forced to tell its tale." It is finally released when the questioners are satisfied. The implicit metaphor is a well-established riddle form. This Mother Goose riddle about a candle is another example:

> Little Nancy Etticoat/In a white petticoat/And a red nose;
> The longer she stands,/The shorter she grows.

Personification—a description of something inanimate as being a living person or animal.

In this riddle the answer, book, is an inanimate object. However it is being personified in all the following ways. It is a prisoner. It tells a tale. He is released after revealing the whole tale.

Pun— is a form of word play that deliberately exploits ambiguity between similar-sounding words for humorous or rhetorical effect.

In this riddle, the following words function as puns for the purpose of misdirection: Bound, tale, and released.

Rhyme—a repetition of similar sounds in two or more words most often used in poetry and songs.

This riddle has the following end-of-line rhymes on the even lines: bound/sound and heard/word. The rhyme scheme is *abcbdefe*.

Meter—is the basic rhythmic structure of a verse.

This riddle is an example of iambic tetrameter followed by iambic trimeter with but one variation (in line 3). Each odd line has four metrical feet, and each even line has three. Each foot is an iamb with the stress on the second syllable. One way to express this is:

      da DUM   da DUM   da DUM   da DUM
      da DUM   da DUM   da DUM

Extra activity: Ask the students to clap this rhythm (soft/loud) as the riddle is read aloud.

Teacher copy of student worksheet

This reference page is designed to show you what the student worksheet looks like.

Sample answers are provided in italics.

The Prisoner

A prisoner he might appear,
Not gagged but strongly bound.
Forced to tell his tale again,
He does and makes no sound.
His questioner just sits and stares
And nothing's ever heard.
He's then released because, in truth,
He's told them every word.

Figuring it out!

Complete the items below:

1. In this riddle the prisoner is not gagged, and yet he tells his tale without making a sound. He communicates every word of his story without ever talking or being talked to. This is very strange. Maybe the prisoner is not a person. In the space below, write a list of ways to communicate a story without speaking.
   sign language, charades, writing, telepathy, art, drawing, painting

2. The riddle says that the prisoner is "strongly bound." If it were a person, one could imagine that the prisoner's hands were tied together, and that maybe he is also tied to a chair or a wall. But if the prisoner is not a person, then "bound" might mean something different from tying a rope around something. In the space below write down all the meanings of the word "bound" that you can think of.
   headed for, tied up, jumping high, bound volume, inevitable

3. If someone releases a prisoner, then he or she might untie the person and let him go. But, if this prisoner is not a person, then maybe there is another way to "release" the prisoner. In the space below, write down different meanings of the word "release."
   letting go, throwing, relaxing, letting someone out of a promise

4. Now, look at all the lists you have written above. If the prisoner is not a person, what can it be?

5. Did you figure it out? If so, what is the answer to this riddle?

Answer: ___*Book*___

For the Teacher

Riddle Title: **The Snake**

> The snake can't ever make them/The shark he never tries,/The eagle prefers not to,/
> And so away he flies./And yet one always finds them/In many climes and lands,/
> A man himself can make them/But never with his hands.

The answer to this riddle is: **<u>Footprints</u>**

This riddle has the following teachable features: Rhyme, and Meter

Rhyme—a repetition of similar sounds in two or more words most often used in poetry and songs.

This riddle has the same word at the end of three lines, so technically it rhymes. The word them refers to the unstated subject of the riddle. Because this is a key theme, it is repeated at the end of the odd-numbered lines one, five, and seven. Its use as a rhyming word, however, is incidental to the overall rhyming structure of the poem—though its presence is an important rhythmic feature. (See the discussion on meter below.)

The poem's structure depends not on these odd-line rhymes, but on the rhymes from the even-numbered lines. The key words from these lines follow. tries/flies, lands/hands. The rhyme scheme is *abcb adad* (The bolded letters indicate the lines which contain rhymes that are critical to the poem's underlying rhyme structure.)

Meter—is the basic rhythmic structure of a verse.

This riddle has a regularly executed meter that is quite interesting. The even lines all are in iambic trimeter. That is they are made up of three metrical feet. Each foot in these lines is an iamb which consists of two syllables; the first being unstressed, and the second stressed (da-DUM).

These lines are each preceded, though, by the odd numbered lines. The odd lines too are made up of three metrical feet, which results in three stressed syllables per line. The even numbered lines, though, have six syllables each, while the odd numbered lines each have seven syllables. The variation of the odd lines comes in the last metrical foot. These lines, then, consist of two iambic feet followed by an amphibrach consisting of a stressed syllable surrounded by two unstressed syllables (da-DUM-da). The amphibrach gives the verse a sing-song quality that increases the relationship between each line pair, and encourages a pause after each pair as this poem is read aloud. The example below shows the last four lines of the poem divided into metrical feet with the stressed syllables bolded.

And	**yet**	one	**al**	ways	**finds**	them
In	**ma**	ny	**climes**	and	**lands**	
A	**man**	him	**self**	can	**make**	them
But	**ne**	ver	**with**	his	**hands**	

Teacher copy of student worksheet

This reference page is designed to show you what the student worksheet looks like.

Sample answers are provided in italics.

The Snake

The snake can't ever make them
The shark he never tries,
The eagle prefers not to,
And so away he flies.
And yet one always finds them
In many climes and lands,
A man himself can make them
But never with his hands.

Figuring it out!

This riddle is about the nature of something. The various clues tell you things that are true about the answer. The trouble is that most of the clues are negative which means they tell you what this thing is not. These pages will help you if you have not already figured out the answer.

Complete the items below:

1. The riddle talks about a snake, a shark, and an eagle. First draw a picture of these three animals in the box below.

2. Whatever they are, the riddle says that the snake can't make them, and the shark never tries. But it also says that the eagle prefers not to. This means that the eagle could make them if he wanted to. Look at the pictures you just drew, and think about the differences between these three animals. In the space below, write down all the ways that an eagle is different from the other two animals.
   an eagle has feathers, talons, a beak, is a bird, can fly, lives high.

3. In the last part of the riddle, it says that man himself can make them but never with his hands. Think about things you can make without using your hands. In the space below, write down anything you can think of that you can make without using your hands.
   goal in soccer, a kick, stomping noise, tracks in the snow, a footprint

4. You can make them, an eagle can make them, but a snake can't. What are they? Did you figure it out?

   If so, what is the answer to this riddle? _**Footprints**_

For the Teacher

Riddle Title: **Steadfast Mates**

You'd think their marriage terribly marred,/She so sharp, and he so hard./And their union doubtless flawed,/Her end pointed, his end clawed./His every action appears abuse,/As he strikes and strikes her without truce./But each, to the other, a steadfast mate,/That, in their congress, goods create./For each is useless when alone,/But both in tandem build a home.

The answer to this riddle is: **<u>Hammer and Nail</u>**

This riddle has the following teachable features: Alliteration, Extended Metaphor, Irony, and Personification.

Alliteration—repetition of the same consonant sound at the beginning of several words in succession.

Examples of alliteration from this riddle include the "m" sound in "marriage terribly marred" from line 1; the "s" sound in "She so sharp" and the "h" sound in "he so hard" from line 2.   The "s" sound in "as he strikes and strikes" (line 6) the "c" in "congress, goods create" (line 8) and the "b" in "But both in tandem build" (line 10) can all be considered examples of alliteration.

Extended Metaphor—establishes a principal comparison and additional comparisons subsidiary to it.

This riddle is an example of an implicit extended metaphor. Rather than explicitly stating that the hammer and the nail are the married couple (and thus revealing the answer) the poet shows ways in which one could think of the attributes of a hammer and nail as similar to those of some married couples. In this case the relationship is shown to be abusive, and yet it endures. The husband/hammer repeatedly strikes wife/nail. Neither spouse is soft, yielding or even appears to be suited for the other. In spite of these appearances (and their physically violent relationship) this married couple can only make a home as partners, never by themselves. The implicit metaphor is a well-established riddle form. This Mother Goose riddle about a cherry is another example:

As I went through the garden gap,/Who should I meet but Dick Redcap!
A stick in his hand, a stone in his throat,/If you'll tell me this riddle, I'll give you a groat.

Irony—is a situation in which there is an incongruity, discordance, or unintended connection with truth, which goes strikingly beyond the most simple and evident meaning of words or actions.

In this riddle, the idea that an abusive relationship makes for a productive team is intentionally ironic. The poet's use of this obvious untruth on the literal level is a clue that can lead to the answer of the riddle. Since it is hard to see how an abusive husband who strikes his wife without truce could contribute to making a home, the listener is invited to think beyond the husband and wife in the human sense.

Personification—a description of something inanimate as being a living person or animal.

In this riddle the answer, hammer and nail, is a set of inanimate objects, but they are being personified in the all following ways. The two are married. His actions are abusive. They are steadfast mates. And together they create goods and build a home.

Teacher copy of student worksheet

This reference page is designed to show you what the student worksheet looks like.

Sample answers are provided in italics.

Steadfast Mates

You'd think their marriage terribly marred,
She so sharp, and he so hard.
And their union doubtless flawed,
Her end pointed, his end clawed.
His every action appears abuse,
As he strikes and strikes her without truce.
But each, to the other, a steadfast mate,
That, in their congress, goods create.
For each is useless when alone,
But both in tandem build a home.

Figuring it out!

The answer to this riddle is not really a married couple, but instead it is a pair of inanimate objects.

Complete the items below:

1. In this riddle the husband is described as having an end that is clawed. He is also described as hard.
   Think of things that are hard and things that have a clawed end. Write down a list of things that
   have one, the other, or both of these characteristics.

   a rock, an eagle, a crowbar, a can opener, a diamond, a cat, armor

2. In this riddle the wife is described as having a pointed end. She is also described as sharp. Think of
   things that are sharp and pointed. Write down a list of things that have these characteristics.

   *toothpick, sword, knife, icepick, spear, arrow, javeline, nail, tack,
   pencil*

3. This husband and wife team built a home. Since they are not people, this does not mean that they
   are interested in the warm and welcoming aspects of a home. Instead it means that they literally
   built a house. In the space below list things that you might use to build a house.

   *wood, glass, doors, windows, drywall, wires, pipes, nails, paint,
   doorknobs*

4. Now look at the lists you have written above. If the husband and wife are not people, what can they
   be? Did you figure it out?

   If so, what is the answer to this riddle? *Hammer and Nail*

For the Teacher

Riddle Title: **Hidden Weapon**

Stars awash in sheen of light/ It calls out loud in vile delight./ Listeners endure in fright./ Vicious brute that reigns at night,/ Evil whelped of heinous bite,/ Renewed by wax, it gains in might./ A leading way to slay the beast,/ Thus hidden weapon is released.

The answer to this riddle is: <u>**Werewolf**</u>

This riddle has the following teachable features: Rhyme, and Meter.

Rhyme—a repetition of similar sounds in two or more words most often used in poetry and songs.

This riddle is technically a series of four rhyming couplets. It appears as a sestet followed by a rhyming couplet, but that is for a sinister reason that will be explained below. A sestet (six line stanza) appears in many rhyme schemes, but it is rare to find one that is *aaaaaa* as this one is. The first six lines all rhyme with each other with the rhyming words light/delight/fright/night/bite/might, this is followed by the rhymes in the final couplet, beast/released. The rhyme scheme can be written *aaaaaabb*.

Meter—is the basic rhythmic structure of a verse.

The basic rhythmic structure of this poem is iambic tetrameter with some variation at the beginning of some lines. Consider line two:

It calls	out loud	in vile	de light
da DUM	da DUM	da DUM	da DUM

The exceptions to this rhythm are notable. In all of the following lines (1, 3, 4, 5, and 6) the poet shortens the initial foot and starts the line with a stress syllable. During a dramatic reading of this poem, this choice lends a sense of growing urgency during the first six lines. The poem then reverts to a faithful adherence to its basic structure in the final rhyming couplet with a calming effect. Notice that each line has four stress syllables with emphasis on the first syllable of the exceptional lines.

Unique features—Unlike most of the riddles in this book, this poem uses descriptive language to set a short scene. The horrifying beast is described in the first six lines and its evident delight is contrasted to the huddled and frightened listeners. There is an abrupt shift from this fell description to a new subject in the final couplet. The last two lines refer to a hidden weapon that is capable of slaying the fearsome beast. But what is it? Where is the weapon hidden?

The weapon is actually hidden in the riddle itself. Remember that this extra clue is not the answer to the riddle, but will help the reader familiar with monster lore to confirm that their answer is correct. The weapon is hidden in the first six lines of the poem, which is why the poem appears as a sestet followed by a separate couplet. (See the discussion of rhyme above.) To find the weapon, one needs to read down the capitalized first letter of each line. Doing this, the reader will find the six-letter word SILVER. The first letters, then, comprise the "leading way" that reveals the traditional weapon used to slay a werewolf.

Teacher copy of student worksheet

This reference page is designed to show you what the student worksheet looks like.

Sample answers are provided in italics.

Hidden Weapon

Stars awash in sheen of light
It calls out loud in vile delight.
Listeners endure in fright.
Vicious brute that reigns at night,
Evil whelped of heinous bite,
Renewed by wax, it gains in might.

A leading way to slay the beast,
Thus hidden weapon is released.

Figuring it out!

Complete the items below:

1. The first six lines of this riddle describe a particular kind of beast. The riddle is set at night and one of the things the beast does is to call out loud. In the space below write down a list of animals that you can think of that make night noises.
   coyote, frog, cricket, wolf, owl, mouse, racoon, possum, nightingale, loon

2. Line six says "Renewed by wax, it gains in might." This means that the beast gets stronger because of wax. But "wax" in this case is not candle wax or beeswax. In the space below write down other meaning of wax.
   the waxing and waning of the moon, someone waxing poetic, ear wax

3. Line five says "Evil whelped of heinous bite." This means that the beast was born because something was bitten. In the space below write down anything you can think of that this line reminds you of.
   a rabid animal turns vicious because of a bite, a wrestler could too

4. The last two lines talk about the hidden weapon that can slay the beast. The weapon is hidden in the first six lines of this riddle in a leading way. What do you notice about the first part of every line in the first six lines? Write down the capital letters of these lines here.
   SILVER

5. What you just wrote down might be the weapon used to slay the beast. What is the beast? Did you figure it out? If so, what is the answer to this riddle?

Answer: *Werewolf*

For the Teacher

Riddle Title: **Mates**

Mates unbalanced,/Or so they seem;/But paired in tandem,/A deadly team./She so gently rounded,/
He so firm and straight,/Yet when they are compounded,/Woe to them they hate.

The answer to this riddle is: **<u>Bow and Arrow</u>**

This riddle has the following teachable features: Metaphor, Personification, and Rhyme.

Metaphor—expressing one thing in terms normally denoting another.

This riddle is an example of an implicit somewhat extended metaphor. Rather than explicitly stating that a bow-and-arrow is a woman-and-man (and thus revealing the answer) the poet shows the many ways that one could think of a bow-and-arrow as having the same attributes as a woman-and-man. They are "mates." She is "gently rounded." He is "firm and straight." They are each part of a team.

Personification—a description of something inanimate as being a living person or animal.

In this riddle, both the bow and the arrow are personified. They are shown to be teammates. They are capable of hate. Because it is a riddle, the poet intentionally creates the impression that the subjects of this verse are actually people, and disguises that fact that they are actually objects personified.

Rhyme—a repetition of similar sounds in two or more words most often used in poetry and songs.

This riddle has an interesting end-of-line rhyme scheme that differs slightly between the stanzas. While the end of line rhymes in the first stanza are on the even lines only (*abcb*). The odd lines and the even lines rhyme in the second stanza (*dede*).   So the rhyme scheme for this poem is *abcb dede*.

Unique Features: The answer to this riddle, instead of being just one thing, is two commonly related objects. In the oral tradition of riddles in English there are other examples of this kind of riddle. Consider this riddle for "sewing with needle and thread":

Old Mrs. Twitchet with her one eye
A tail of wondrous length lets fly.
Every time she goes through the gap
She leaves a piece of her tail in a trap

Or this riddle for "tongue and teeth:"

Sixteen white sheep standing in the stall,
Great big red sheep looks over them all.

Teacher copy of student worksheet
This reference page is designed to show you what the student worksheet looks like.
Sample answers are provided in italics.

<u>Mates</u>

Mates unbalanced,
Or so they seem;
But paired in tandem,
A deadly team.

She so gently rounded,
He so firm and straight,
Yet when they are compounded,
Woe to them they hate.

Figuring it out!

Complete the items below:

1. In this riddle, the answer is actually two things instead of just one. They are paired as part of a team. These are things that commonly go together like peanut-butter and jelly or salt and pepper. In the space below, write a list of things that commonly go together:
   hammer and nails, cheese and crackers, leather and lace, night and day, desk and chair, pencil and paper, cats and dogs, horse and rider, bread and butter, peaches and cream, washer and dryer

   Look at what you just wrote. Are any of these things "deadly"?

2. The two team members in this riddle are very different from each other. "She" is described as gently rounded. "He" is described as firm and straight. But the two things that make up the answer are not people or animals. Instead they are inanimate objects. In the spaces below write a list of things you can think of that are rounded, and then a list of things that are firm and straight.
   Rounded→ ball, wheel, meatball, dough, pellets, pebbles
   Straight→ rifle barrel, sword, knife, ruler, straight razor, arrow

3. These two things form a "deadly team." Neither one alone is very dangerous, but when used together they can be deadly. In the space below, write a list of things that you can think of that are deadly.
   guns, knives, swords, spears, bow and arrows, catpult, bombs

Look at what you just wrote. Are any of these deadly things made up of two parts? Could one part be called rounded while the other part is straight?

4. Did you figure it out? If so, what is the answer to this riddle? *Bow and Arrow*

For the Teacher

Riddle Title: **Do Me In**

Do me in to do the law/So you can do me out./Do me through, do me to ground,/Give me away, you lout./ Do me down or do me up/But up I'll get a heart./Do me when you are in camp/To get an early start./ Do me fast when I'm the day,/So fast I get a neck./Do me even, to a horse,/Take five - Oh what the heck.

The answer to this riddle is: **Break**

This riddle has the following teachable features: Compound Words, Rhyme, and Ballad Stanza.

Compound Words—are made when two words are joined to form a new word.

This highly linguistic riddle depends, for its solution, on several language-related clues. One of these is the use of the incomplete compound word. There are five examples of this type of clue. They are *through*, *down*, *up*, *fast* and *neck*. One type of traditional logic puzzle provides a list, like this one, of clue words. The solver is to provide the one missing word such that when it is joined to all of these it results in a list of legitimate compound words. In this case the correct word is the word "break." Adding "break" will result in this list: breakthrough, breakdown, breakup, breakfast. and breakneck.

For an amusing additional exercise, have your students write down a list of compound words from their own experience where one of the parts of the compound is common to all words. (e.g., "*house*hold," "*house*top," "work*house*," and "play*house*"). Then they should rewrite their list but remove the common word (i.e., hold, top, work, & play). Now they can exchange their list with another student and see if their partner can figure out one word to add that will successfully turn the list into a series of legitimate compound words.

Rhyme—a repetition of similar sounds in two or more words most often used in poetry and songs.

This riddle has the following end-of-line rhymes: out/lout, heart/start, and neck/heck. The rhyme scheme is *abcb defe ghih* in three four-line stanzas.

Ballad Stanza—is the four-line stanza, known as a quatrain, most often found in the folk ballad. This form consists of alternating four- and three-stress lines. Usually only the second and fourth lines rhyme (in an *abcb* pattern).

This riddle is written in a ballad stanza form with alternating seven and six syllable lines. The longer are four-stress lines, and the shorter are three-stress lines. The bold syllables of the first stanza reproduced below show the stress pattern.

Do me **in** to **do** the **law**/So **you** can **do** me **out**.

Do me **through**, do **me** to **ground**,/Give **me** a — **way**, you **lout**.

Famous works that have this kind of stress pattern (but with 8- and 6-syllable alternating lines) include the poem "The Rime of the Ancient Mariner" by Samuel Taylor Coleridge, and the Christian hymn "Amazing Grace" by John Newton.

To bring this lesson home, have the students clap the rhythm while the riddle is read aloud.

Teacher copy of student worksheet

This reference page is designed to show you what the student worksheet looks like.

Sample answers are provided in italics.

<u>Do Me In</u>

Do me in to do the law
So you can do me out.
Do me through, do me to ground,
Give me away, you lout.

Do me down or do me up
But up I'll get a heart.
Do me when you are in camp
To get an early start.

Do me fast when I'm the day,
So fast I get a neck.
Do me even, to a horse,
Take five - Oh what the heck.

Figuring it out!

Complete the items below:

1. In this who am I riddle, the answer is a word that can often take the place of the words *do me*. There are 15 words that are clues, but the clues are of different types. In one type of clue, the answer is one part of a compound word. In the spaces below, fill in the blank with any word you can think of that will turn each answer into a regular English compound word.   For example, if the clue was "_____ house" you might write work*house* or you might write play*house*:

fall   through, fall down,   throw up,   break fast, rubber neck

Look at the words you just wrote. Could any one of them fit in all the spaces above?

2. When people sleep at a campsite during a long hike, they need to pack up before they continue the hike. In the space below, write different ways of describing these actions.

get an early start, take down the tent, stuff the pack, break camp

3. When people violate the law, they can get in trouble. In the space below write different ways of saying "violate the law."

break the law, commit a crime, offense, misdemeanor, felony

4. When people "take five," it means that they take a rest from what they were doing. In the space below, write different ways of saying take a rest.

stop for coffee, take a break, take a nap, siesta, time out, relax

5.   Did you figure it out? If so, what is the answer to this riddle?   *Break*

For the Teacher

Riddle Title: **My Cross**

Since he was cross, and I was cross,/We crossed across the field./
I crossed my cross across his cross/To try to make him yield./So toe to toe we both did go/
And crossed our crosses fell./When my cross crossed across his cross/It clanged just like a bell./
What is my cross, what is his cross/That crisscrossed through the air?/
Now don't get cross if you can't guess./It is my cross to bare.

The answer to this riddle is: **<u>Sword</u>**

This riddle has the following teachable features: Pun, Alliteration, Assonance, Consonance, Ballad Stanza, Simile, Onomatopoeia, and Rhyme.

Pun— is a form of word play that deliberately exploits ambiguity between similar-sounding words for humorous or rhetorical effect.

In the last line "It is my cross to bare" the word "bare" is intended to throw off the listener who will assume, because of the common expression, that the word was meant to be "bear." But the pun is a clue to the answer because to bare a sword is to unsheathe it.

Alliteration—Repetition of the same consonant sound at the beginning of several words in succession.

In line 4 of this poem, the words "<u>T</u>o <u>t</u>ry <u>t</u>o.."" is an example of alliteration as is "...<u>c</u>ross <u>c</u>rossed across his <u>c</u>ross" from line 7.

Assonance—a refrain of vowel sounds to create internal rhyming within phrases.

Line 5 "S<u>o</u> t<u>oe</u> to t<u>oe</u> we b<u>o</u>th did g<u>o</u>" is a strong example of assonance.

Consonance—repetition of the same consonant sound within a phrase.

This poem has many examples of consonance. A few prime examples include: Line 3 "I <u>cr</u>ossed my <u>cr</u>oss a<u>cr</u>oss his <u>cr</u>oss" and line 4 "<u>T</u>o <u>t</u>ry <u>t</u>o make him yield."

Ballad Stanza—is the four-line stanza, known as a quatrain, most often found in the folk ballad. This form consists of alternating four- and three-stress lines. Usually only the second and fourth lines rhyme (in an abcb pattern).

This riddle is written in a ballad stanza form with alternating eight and six syllable lines. The longer are four-stress lines, and the shorter are three-stress lines. The bold syllables of the first stanza reproduced below show the stress pattern.

Since **he** was ***cross***, and ***I*** was ***cross***,/We ***crossed*** a**cross** the ***field***.
I ***crossed*** my ***cross*** a**cross** his ***cross***/To ***try*** to ***make*** him ***yield***.

To bring this lesson home, have the students clap the rhythm while the poem is read aloud.

Simile—a comparison between two unlike things using the word "like" or "as"

In this poem, the clang that two swords make is "...***like*** a bell" (line 8)

Onomatopoeia—a word formed by imitation of a sound made by its referent.

The word "clanged" in line 8 is an example of onomatopoeia.

Rhyme—a repetition of similar sounds in two or more words most often used in poetry and songs.

This riddle has the following end-of-line rhymes: cross/cross, field/yield, fell/bell, air/bare. The important rhymes to the underlying structure are at the end of the even lines. The rhyme scheme for this poem is abab, *cdad, aefe.*

Teacher copy of student worksheet
This reference page is designed to show you what the student worksheet looks like.
Sample answers are provided in italics.

My Cross

Since he was cross, and I was cross,
We crossed across the field.
I crossed my cross across his cross
To try to make him yield.
So toe to toe we both did go
And crossed our crosses fell.

When my cross crossed across his cross
It clanged just like a bell.
What is my cross, what is his cross
That crisscrossed through the air?
Now don't get cross if you can't guess.
It is my cross to bare.

Figuring it out!

"What is my cross?" the riddle asks. The answer to this riddle is not a cross. It is something that, in some ways, is like a cross. To answer this riddle correctly you need to figure out what the "cross" really is.

Complete the items below:

1. The word "cross" in the first line means angry or mad. Sometimes you can tell when people are angry by their actions. In the space below write a list of things that people do that show that they are angry.
   kick things, throw things, hit things, yell, scream, fight, turn red

2. The speaker of the poem is trying to make someone else "yield" or give up. The two of them ("he" and "I") are in some kind of fight. In the space below make a list of all the different ways you can think of that people fight.
   boxing, wrestling, gun fights, knife fights, yelling, kicking

3. At the end of the second stanza, the riddle says "When my cross crossed across his cross it clanged just like a bell." In the box below, draw a picture of what might be going on.

4. Notice the spelling of "bare" in the last line. To bare something means to uncover it. In the space below make a list of all things that you would uncover in order to fight with them.

   take off gloves, draw a gun, unsheathe a sword or knife

5. Did you figure out what the cross actually is?
   If so, what is the answer to this riddle? *Sword*

For the Teacher

Riddle Title: **Aphrodite**

> A gruesome traveler, mud bemired,/Approaches here all worn and tired./Upon the spot a trim bed makes,/And of her rest she then partakes./Her silken sheets she wraps so tight,/They quite conceal her from my sight./Now oft' before I've heard it said,/That beauty marred is healed in bed./ But to me such talk was cheap,/I've not believed in beauty sleep./Until I saw this traveler wake,/ And she her silken bed forsake./Who went to bed at best untidy,/Arose at length an Aphrodite.

The answer to this riddle is: **Butterfly** (Alternate answers are *caterpillar* and *moth*)

This riddle has the following teachable features: Consonance, Metaphor, Personification, Rhyming Couplets, Internal Rhyme, and Meter.

Consonance—is a stylistic poetic device characterized by the repetition of the same consonant two or more times in short succession.

In this riddle, consider the "s" sound in the line: 'Her **s**ilken **sh**eet**s sh**e wrap**s s**o tight" as an example of consonance.

Metaphor—expressing one thing in terms normally denoting another.

This riddle is an example of an implicit somewhat extended metaphor. Rather than explicitly stating that a caterpillar/butterfly is a traveler getting beauty sleep (and thus revealing the answer) the poet shows how caterpillar/butterfly can be thought of in terms of a female human traveler. She arrives "mud bemired" from her travels, goes to bed in silken sheets, and wakes up transformed by beauty sleep.

Personification—a description of something inanimate as being a living person or animal.

In this riddle the butterfly is an animal personified because it is given human qualities. It makes its own bed. It uses silk sheets. It partakes of beauty sleep, and it resembles Aphrodite when it wakens.

Rhyming couplets—a couplet is a pair of lines of verse. It usually consists of two lines that rhyme and have the same meter.

Consider the meter of lines five and six:

> Her **silk** — en **sheets** she **wraps** so **tight**,
> They **quite** con — **ceal** her **from** my **sight**.

Internal Rhyme—or "middle rhyme" is rhyme that occurs in a single line of verse.

In the example couplet above, the words "quite" and "sight" are an example of internal rhyme.

Meter— is the basic rhythmic structure of a verse.

This riddle is an example of iambic tetrameter with some variation. The couplet copied above is a good example. Each line has four metrical feet, and each is an iamb with the stress on the second syllable. One way to express this for each line is:

da DUM   da DUM   da DUM   da DUM

Teacher copy of student worksheet

This reference page is designed to show you what the student worksheet looks like.

Sample answers are provided in italics.

Aphrodite

A gruesome traveler, mud bemired,
Approaches here all worn and tired.
Upon the spot a trim bed makes,
And of her rest she then partakes.
Her silken sheets she wraps so tight,
They quite conceal her from my sight.

Now oft' before I've heard it said,
That beauty marred is healed in bed.
But to me such talk was cheap,
I've not believed in beauty sleep.
Until I saw this traveler wake,
And she her silken bed forsake.
Who went to bed at best untidy,
Arose at length an Aphrodite.

Figuring it out!

Complete the items below:

1. To answer this riddle you need to say who the "gruesome traveler" is. The riddle tells us that she arrives and goes to bed in "silken sheets." Why do you suppose the sheets are silk? In the space below write down what you know about how silk is made.
   Silk production started in China. Silkworm cocoons are used.

2. Aphrodite is the name of the Greek goddess of love and beauty. So the riddle tells us that the traveler goes to bed looking gruesome and muddy, but wakes up beautiful. The answer to the riddle is not a person, but is, instead, something found in nature. In the space below write down things you can think of that undergo transformations in nature.
   tadpoles become frogs, caterpillars become moths

   Look at what you just wrote. Do any of these transformations begin ugly, and end up beautiful?

3. The riddle tells us that the gruesome traveler wraps her silken sheets in a way that actually conceals her. After she emerges, she is beautiful. Think of a chick emerging from an egg. What other things in nature can you think of that emerge from a hiding place? In the space below, write down a list of the things you can think of in nature that emerge from a tight hiding place.
   a mole underground, a turtle in a shell, a butterfly in a cocoon.

4. What is the answer to this riddle? ___*Butterfly*___

For the Teacher

Riddle Title: **Lustrous Beauty**

Behold the lustrous beauty of my bride./The colors of the night shine in her skin./I long for arms to hold her to my side;/In truth this game is one I ne'er can win./And wed were we as day turned into night./ She held a pure bouquet of whitest flour./Her dress was red and I was tawny white./Our ceremony took but half an hour./My bride was born to be Baba Ghanoush;/While mother mine was but a lowly cow./ My wife had grown up looking like a bush/So is my bride not known to you by now?/ Though she was grown and raised by Farmer John,/Our married surname now is Parmesan.

The answer to this riddle is: **Eggplant**

This riddle has the following teachable features: Extended Metaphor, Rhyme, Meter, Pun, and Sonnet

Extended Metaphor—establishes a principal comparison and additional comparisons subsidiary to it.

In this riddle, the eggplant is a bride, but then the riddle goes on to talk about the preparation of the meal (eggplant Parmesan) in terms of a wedding ceremony. All of these details (the bouquet, the half-hour ceremony, the color of dress, and the change of name) extend the original metaphor that the eggplant is actually married to Parmesan, the big cheese.

Rhyme—a repetition of similar sounds in two or more words most often used in poetry and songs.

This riddle has the following end-of-line rhymes: bride/side, skin/win, night/white, flour/hour, Ganoush/ bush, cow/now, and John/Parmesan. This riddle is in the form of a Shakespearean sonnet so its rhyme scheme is (*abab, cdcd, efef, gg*)

Meter—is the basic rhythmic structure of a verse.

The poem is written in iambic pentameter with no variations. This means that each line is exactly 10 syllables long with the stress on the even syllables. That is there are five metrical feet (pentameter). Each foot (in this case an iamb) is of two syllables where the first is unstressed and the second stressed. (da-DUM).

Sample Iambic Pentameter Rhythm from "Lustrous Beauty"

1	2	3	4	5
da DUM	da DUM	da DUM	da DUM	da DUM
Be **hold**	the **lus**	trous **beau**	ty **of**	my **bride**

Pun— is a form of word play that deliberately exploits ambiguity between similar-sounding words for humorous or rhetorical effect.

In this riddle the word "flour" is intended to throw off the listener who will assume that word was meant to be "flower." However, written, this word acts as clue to the identity of the lustrous beauty and could serve to help the solver start thinking the right way.

Sonnet—is a fourteen-line poem that follows a strict rhyme scheme and specific structure.

Sonnets come in several popular variations. Lustrous Beauty is a Shakespearean sonnet which means that it is written in iambic pentameter (see Meter above) and has the rhyme scheme of *abab, cdcd, efef, gg*. That is, it is made up of three quatrains (four line stanzas), followed by a rhyming couplet (of two lines).

Isn't this one romantic?

Teacher copy of student worksheet

This reference page is designed to show you what the student worksheet looks like.

Sample answers are provided in italics.

Lustrous Beauty

Behold the lustrous beauty of my bride.
The colors of the night shine in her skin.
I long for arms to hold her to my side;
In truth this game is one I ne'er can win.

And wed were we as day turned into night.
She held a pure bouquet of whitest flour.
Her dress was red and I was tawny white.
Our ceremony took but half an hour.

My bride was born to be Baba Ghanoush;
While mother mine was but a lowly cow.
My wife had grown up looking like a bush
So is my bride not known to you by now?

Though she was grown and raised by Farmer John,
Our married surname now is Parmesan.

Figuring it out!

Complete the items below:

1. The answer to this riddle is the name of the bride. But the bride and the bridegroom are not people. Listing things that the riddle tells you about the bridegroom and the bride may help you solve this riddle. In the spaces below list the things the riddle tells you about the bridegroom and the bride.
   Bridegroom—has no arms, is tawny white, mother = cow, Parmesan
   Bride—dark skin, holds white flour, wears red, Baba Ghanoush, bush

2. At the end of line six is the word 'flour' instead of the word 'flower.' This word is not a mistake in spelling, instead it tells you a great deal about the nature of the bride and groom. In the space below write down things you associate with the word 'flour'
   bread, baking, food, white, ingredient, powdery, soft, comes in bags

3. The "wedding" in the riddle is not a real wedding, but it stands for these two objects coming together to form a sort of union. Given what you have written above, what kinds of things are the bride and groom, and what happened during the half-hour wedding?
   Groom = cheese, bride = plant, wedding = cooking them together.

4. Did you figure out what the bride actually is?

If so, what is the answer to this riddle? *Eggplant*

For the Teacher

Riddle Title: **The Strange House**

This house holds rooms, one score and six,/That shelter a vast mob./It lets lions lie down with the lambs,/ Yet makes both shun the slob./None now will nestle with nicks and nates,/While reams room near the rear./Though you and I have separate rooms/Both our bottles brim with beer./The king and queen can never mate/(Though hands and hearts hobnob)/Because their rooms are separate/If this jail does its job./ What house is this that rules thus/Forcing faith to fend with fear?/ The answer to this riddle lies/With dead and dying here.

The answer to this riddle is: **<u>Dictionary</u>**

This riddle has the following teachable features: Alliteration, Extended Metaphor, Rhyme, and Ballad Stanza,

Alliteration—repetition of the same consonant sound at the beginning of several words in succession.

This poem is chock full of alliteration. Take the "n" sound in line five as an example: "None now will nestle with nicks and nates." In this line every stressed syllable begins with the "n" sound. Other examples of heavy alliteration in this poem include lines 1, 3, 6, 8, 10, 12, 14 and 16. One obvious reason that most of the lines in this poem are so strongly alliterative has to do with the fact that the answer is dictionary. Dictionary's, after all, group words together by first letter.

Extended Metaphor—establishes a principle comparison and additional comparisons subsidiary to it.

In this poem, The central implicit metaphor is that a dictionary is a house. This metaphorical construct is extended throughout the poem which describes various "rooms" and their contents, and also talks about the prison-like nature of this house that prevents the dwellers of one room to inhabit any other.

Rhyme—a repetition of similar sounds in two or more words most often used in poetry and songs.

This riddle has the following end-of-line rhymes: mob/slob, rear/beer, hobnob/job, and fear/hear. (Lines nine and eleven end with a half-rhyme mate/separate, but this rhyme, while satisfying, is not required of the rhyme scheme). This poem is written in ballad stanza form (see the Ballad Stanza section below) and so the rhyme scheme is (*abcb, defe, ghih, jklk*) where within each of the four quatrains the even lines rhyme.

Ballad Stanza—is the four-line stanza, known as a quatrain, most often found in the folk ballad. This form consists of alternating four- and three-stress lines. Usually only the second and fourth lines rhyme (in an *abcb* pattern).

This riddle is written in a ballad stanza form with alternating eight and six syllable lines (with several slight variations). The longer are four-stress lines, and the shorter are three-stress lines. The bold syllables of the last two lines reproduced below show this stress pattern.

The **an** — swer **to** this **rid** — dle **lies**

With **dead** and **dy** — ing **here**.

Teacher copy of student worksheet
This reference page is designed to show you what the student worksheet looks like.
Sample answers are provided in *italics.*

The Strange House

This house holds rooms, one score and six,
That shelter a vast mob.
It lets lions lie down with the lambs,
Yet makes both shun the slob.
None now will nestle with nicks and nates,
While reams room near the rear.
Though you and I have separate rooms
Both our bottles brim with beer.

The king and queen can never mate
(Though hands and hearts hobnob)
Because their rooms are separate
If this jail does its job.
What house is this that rules thus
Forcing faith to fend with fear?
The answer to this riddle lies
With dead and dying here.

Figuring it out!

The answer to this riddle is a single, inanimate object with many things inside. Looking

at the clues in the riddle will help you figure out what that one thing might be

Complete the items below:

1. The number of rooms in this house is "one score and six." A score is equal to twenty, so this house
   has twenty-six rooms. What does twenty-six remind you of? In the space below write down a list
   of things you associate with the number twenty-six.
   alphabet, weeks in half a year, half a deck of cards, 26th amendment

2. In line three, the strange house "…lets lions lie down with the lambs." What do lions have in
   common with lambs? In the space below write down everything you think lions and lambs have in
   common.
   both animals, have four legs, mammals, start with l, end with s.

3. In line five we find that "None now will nestle with nicks and nates," Look at the words in this line.
   In the space below, write down what many of these words have in common?
   five of the eight words start with the letter n. two start with w.

4. In line fourteen, the house is "Forcing faith to fend with fear." Look at the words in this line. In the
   space below, write down what many of these words have in common?
   four of the six words start with the letter f.

5. Look at your responses to items 1-4 above. See if you can find any similarities. Now look at the
   whole riddle. In the space below, write down any pattern you notice about the words in this riddle
   that are assigned to the same room in this very strange house.
   many of the rooms have words that start with the same letter.

6. Did you figure out what this strange house could be?

If so, what is the answer to this riddle? *Dictionary*

For the Teacher

Riddle Title: **Cyclops**

>A cyclops stares from pale white face./Earrings seven his visage grace./Atop his head are five
tattoos./Ebon black his pair of shoes./On his pale back six scars dug deep./He felt no pain
and did not weep./His job to tumble, bounce and fall;/But he's no fool. No not at all!

The answer to this riddle is: **six-sided die**

This riddle has the following teachable features: Consonance, Metaphor, Personification, Rhyme, and Meter.

Consonance—repetition of the same consonant sound within a phrase.

Consider the "s" sound from lines one and two: "A cyclops stares from pale white face/Earrings seven his visage grace." In line five there are two alliterative pairs. Consider the four "s" sounds in quick succession in the first of these: "six scars." This followed immediately by the second alliterative pair repeating the "d" sound: "dug deep."

Metaphor—expressing one thing in terms normally denoting another.

The first five lines of this riddle comprise an extended metaphor that, when the parts are taken together, describes the pips on a six-sided die. The single pip face is represented by the face of the cyclops with his single eye. The two pips are the ebon black pair of shoes. The three- and four-pip side are deduced by the cyclops' "seven" earrings. The five-pip side is metaphorically represented by the tattoos. Finally the six scars dug deep into the back of the cyclops metaphorically represent the six-pip side of the die. Because this is a riddle, the faces of the die are never stated, but are instead metaphorically implied. The listener must deduce the unspoken part of this extended metaphor in order to solve the riddle.

Personification—a description of something inanimate as being a living person or animal.

In this riddle the answer, six-sided die, is an inanimate object. However it is being personified as a fully described cyclops. The single eye is implied, and may require background knowledge, but once that is known, the idea is that the various parts of the three-dimensional cyclops (eye, earrings, shoes, tattoos, and scars) correspond exactly to the relative positions of the pips on a standard six-sided die.

Rhyme—a repetition of similar sounds in two or more words most often used in poetry and songs.

The four rhyming couplets of his riddle have the following end-of-line rhymes: face/grace, tattoos/shoes, deep/weep, fall/all. The rhyme scheme is *aabb ccdd*.

Meter—is the basic rhythmic structure of a verse.

With the exceptions of lines 2 and 4, each line of this poem is written in iambic tetrameter. That is, there are four metrical feet of two syllables each with the stress on the second syllable (da-DUM). However there is an interestingly clipped cadence in the first foot of each of these lines as the reader is rushed to the stressed syllable in every case. As for the exceptional lines, line two starts with two trochees (DUM-da) followed by two iambs. (The occasional use of a trochee is a common variation to iambic rhythmic structure.) Line 4 has only seven syllables rather than the expected eight. This line lacks the first (unstressed) syllable of the first foot. This is called headless verse and is another common variation to poetic rhythm in English verse.

Teacher copy of student worksheet

This reference page is designed to show you what the student worksheet looks like.

Sample answers are provided in italics.

<u>Cyclops</u>

A cyclops stares from pale white face.
Earrings seven his visage grace.
Atop his head are five tattoos.
Ebon black his pair of shoes.
On his pale back six scars dug deep.
He felt no pain and did not weep.
His job to tumble, bounce and fall;
But he's no fool. No not at all!

Figuring it out!

This riddle is an "I saw" riddle. The "cyclops" is being described by the speaker of the riddle, but the cyclops himself is not the speaker. The thing being described is actually an inanimate object that in some ways is like a cyclops. The job of the solver of the riddle is to figure out what is really being described here.

Complete the items below:

There are quite a few numbers that are in this riddle. Some of the obvious ones are seven, five, and six, but there are other numbers implied. Even though a cyclops has **one** eye, he probably has **two** ears, so when you fill in the numbers below, divide the earrings in such a way as they are not all on one ear. In each space below, write in one numeral that you think best answers the question:

1. How many eyes does the cyclops have? *1*

2. How many shoes does the cyclops have? *2*

3. How many earrings are on the cyclops' left ear? *3*

4. How many earrings are on the cyclops' right ear? *4*

5. How many tattoos are on the cyclops' head? *5*

6. How many scars are on the cyclops' back? *6*

7. The riddle uses the word "pale" twice. First describing the cyclops' face, and then describing his back. Considering these clues, guess the color of the cyclops' skin. *white*

8. The riddle also uses the phrase "ebon black" when describing the shoes. If we extend this idea to include everything else, what color would all these items be? *black*

9. Draw the cyclops as described in this poem:

10. Did you figure it out what the cyclops actually is?

If so, what is the answer to this riddle? *six-sided die*

Student Worksheets

The following pages contain the studen worksheets. Permission is hereby granted to copy this by an individual teacher for classroom use. All other rights are reserved.

To get printable copies in PDF format, please visit:

www.cloudkingdom.com/RIALAC

<u>Never Orange</u>

I'm never orange,
Though yellow can be.
A bard's good friend,
In his songs you find me.

In a child's book kept,
And in ballads too,
I'll bet you're surprised
Not to find me right here.

Figuring it out!

This is an "I am" riddle where the speaker is the answer to the riddle. The job of the solver is to figure out what the "I" is that is speaking the riddle. It is not a person.

Complete the items below:

1. A bard is the same as a poet. Bards of old would sing or recite epic or heroic poetry. Imagine that a bard was singing to you. What kinds of things might you find in his songs? In the space below write down as many features of songs as you can think of.

____

____

____

<u>Continue</u> ⟹

2. The answer to this riddle, whatever it is, is kept in a child's book. Children's books have some typical features. In the space below write down a list of features that are common in books for very young children.

____

____

____

3. A ballad is a simple song that tells a story. Ballads usually have a melody line that repeats as the story is told. There are many popular songs that are called ballads like "American Pie" and "The Ballad of Billy the Kid." Imagine that you were asked to write a ballad. In the space below, write a list of things you would be sure to include in your ballad.

____

____

____

4. The last lines of this riddle say" I'll bet your surprised not to find me right here." Given your answers to the questions above, what might one expect to find at the end of the last line that is missing?

____

5. Did you figure it out? If so, what is the answer to this riddle?

Answer: _____________________________________

Shooting Rays

Rays shoot from its heart
Spoke silently without words
Fastest when tired.

Figuring it out!

Complete the items below:

1. This riddle is only three lines long, but that does not mean it is easy to solve. In the first line "Rays shoot from its heart" the word "heart" does not mean the beating machine that pumps blood in a person or an animal. Think of other meanings of the word heart and write them in the space below.

____

____

____

2. The phrase "rays shoot" begins the first line of this riddle, but this is not some kind of death ray that someone is shooting. There are other meanings to the word "rays" apart from the sun's rays, or laser beams. Furthermore these "rays" are not intended to be aimed at anyone or shot at anyone. In the space below, write other possible meanings of the phrase "rays shoot."

____

____

____

<u>Continue</u> ⟹

3. The word "spoke" in the second line does not refer to someone who was talking. Can you
   think of anything else that could be meant by the word spoke? In the space below write
   down any other meanings of the word spoke that you can think of.

____

____

____

4. The word "tired" in the third line does not refer to fatigue. It has nothing to do with being
   exhausted at all. Can you think of any other meanings for the word tired? Write them
   down in the space below.

____

____

____

5. Did you figure it out? If so, what is the answer to this riddle?

Answer: ____

The Oracle

Eastern oracle
Conceals the future within
A light and sweet cave.

Figuring it out!

Complete the items below:

1. This riddle is only three lines long, but that does not mean it is easy to solve. The first line "Eastern oracle" contains the word oracle. An oracle is a person or place that is a source of wise counsel and accurate predictions of the future. Palm readers and Ouija boards are considered by some to be modern oracles. In the space below, write out a list of things that are supposed to be able to predict the future.

____

____

____

2. The word cave evokes images of a dark place where things can hide (or be hidden). Caves are not generally thought of as "light" and "sweet," but the cave in the riddle is described as both. In the spaces below, list things that are light in weight, and then things that are sweet.

Things that are light →
____

Things that are sweet ›
____

<u>Continue</u> ▯▯⇒

3. The answer to this riddle is something that hides (conceals) the future in a light and sweet and dark place (cave). Suppose you knew the future, and you wanted to hide what you knew in something light and sweet. In the space below describe what you would do.

____

____

____

____

____

____

____

____

4. Did you figure it out? If so, what is the answer to this riddle?

Answer: _______________________________________

<u>The Traveler</u>

Travels by whispers
Or else its death is certain
Passageway concealed

Figuring it out!

Complete the items below:

1. This riddle is made up of two different clues. The first clue is in the first two lines. Whatever the answer to this riddle is, it is a thing that can only travel by whispers or else it is sure to be destroyed. In the space below write down things you would need to whisper:

____

____

____

2. The second clue is in the third line. It says passageway concealed. This clue is a slightly different way to think about the one-word answer to this riddle. In the space below write down as many different words you can think of that mean the same thing as the word "concealed."

____

____

____

<u>Continue</u> ⟹

Look back at what you just wrote for both numbers one and two on the previous page. Are there any words that are on both your lists?

3. Did you figure it out? If so, what is the answer to this riddle?

Answer: ________________________________

Friendly Ghost

Ghostly companion!
Flat black mirror of your soul.
Partner eternal.

Figuring it out!

Complete the items below:

1. The answer to this short riddle is one word. It is described as both a companion and a partner. In the space below write down all the qualities that you find in a ***companion***, and then the qualities you find in a ***partner***. This will help you discover some qualities shared by the answer to this riddle, so do not worry if some of the words on these two lists are the same.

Companion →

____

____

Partner →

____

____

2. Mirrors are funny things. They enable you to see things you cannot touch, taste, hear, or smell. In the space below write a description of what you would see in a mirror if you crossed a room while looking at it.

____

____

Continue ⇨

3. The answer to this riddle is also described as ghostly. In the space below write down as
   many qualities of a ghost as you can think of.

____

____

____

4. The ghost in this riddle is different from the white ghosts one might see on Halloween.
   This ghost is described as both black and flat. Imagine a black ghost walking around that
   is also as flat as a pancake! In the space below, write down a list of things that are both flat
   and black.

____

____

____

5. So, we have something that is like a companion and loyal partner that shares some qualities
   of a mirror, and is a flat black ghost. Did you figure it out? If so, what is the answer to this
   riddle?

Answer: _______________________________________

By the Road

Board by the road
On the face of a duck
A check is now due
Folded, where cash is stuck

Figuring it out!

Complete the items below:

1. The answer to this riddle is a word that has multiple meanings. The clues in this puzzle hint at the different meanings of the word. The first line "Board by the road" is hinting at one meaning of the answer. In the space below, list as many kinds of "boards" as you can think of. Especially think about "boards" that you can see from the road.

____

____

____

2. The second line talks about the face of a duck. In the box below see if you can draw the face of a duck.

Can you name the different parts of the face? List the parts of a duck's face here:

____

____

____

Continue ⇒

3. The third line says that "A check is now due." This means that someone needs to write a check in order to pay a debt. What do you pay with a check? Can you think of words associated with writing checks? List them below.

____

____

____

4. The last line says "Folded where cash is stuck." In the space below, write a list of places where people keep their cash? Can you think of one that contains the word "fold"?

____

____

____

5. Look over your work on this sheet. Can you find any words that are common across your answers to the questions above?

____

6. Did you figure it out? If so, what is the answer to this riddle?

Answer: ___________________________________

Short fingers

Halo of water, tongue of wood
Skin of stone, long I've stood.
My fingers short reach to the sky
Inside my heart men live and die.

Figuring it out!

Complete the items below:

1. This is an "I am" riddle. The speaker is an inanimate object, but it is still describing itself. What the solver needs to do is figure out who is speaking by what is being described. The riddle starts with the words "Halo of water." What can that mean? In the space below, write down everything you know about a halo.

____

____

____

2. The next thing the riddle says is tongue of wood. What can that mean? In the space below write down a list of things that can be made out of wood. HINT: your list can include big things as well as little things.

____

____

____

____

<u>Continue</u>

3. The next thing the riddle says is skin of stone. What can that mean? In the space below,
   write down things that are made so that the outside layer is stone.

____

____

____

4. Putting this together, the speaker of this riddle has a watery halo, a wooden tongue, stone
   skin, and short fingers that reach up. It also has room enough for men to live and die in
   its heart. How can one thing have all these features? In the box below, draw a picture of
   something that has all these things.

5. Did you figure it out? If so, what is the answer to this riddle?

Answer: ______________________________________

NAME: _______________________________

Not a Kite

Though not a kite, it needs a wind.
Pull on its arm, it does not mind.
Upon large rocks it likes to sup,
But every time it throws them up.

Figuring it out!

This riddle is an "I saw" riddle. The thing being described by the speaker is the answer to the riddle.

The job of the solver is to figure out what is actually being described.

Complete the items below:

1. The first line ends with the word wind. However, since this is a rhyming verse, we find out by looking at the end of the second line that the correct pronunciation needs to rhyme with the word mind. So we have the verb wind (like to wind up a kite string) rather than noun wind (like the moving air that keeps the kite flying). Apart from kite string, other things need to be wound. In the spaces below, first make a short list of things you can think of that need to be wound. Then describe why you think things need to be wound.

Things that need to be wound—

____

____

Why things need to be wound—

____

____

Continue ⫿⇒

2. The third line tells us that this thing likes to sup (eat) large rocks. Think of things that are capable of lifting up large rocks. In the space below, write down a list of things that you associate with lifting large rocks. HINT: Don't limit your list to only things that are used in the present day construction site.

____

____

3. The fourth line tells us that every time this things sups on large rocks, it throws them up.   In the space below, write down a list of everything you can think of that is capable of throwing large rocks up into the air.

____

____

4. Look at what you wrote above and then read the riddle again. Did you figure it out? If so, what is the answer to this riddle?

____

<u>Anger</u>

Anger, cowardice and envy
Appear to be just base emotions,
But overhead they guide your feet
And stipulate your forward motions.

Figuring it out!

The answer to this riddle is a single inanimate object that is made up of three significant parts. To solve this riddle, you need to figure out what anger, cowardice, and envy represent.

Complete the items below:

1. Anger is the first emotion in this riddle. In the space below, write down a list of all the things that you associate with anger.

____

____

____

2. Cowardice is the second emotion on the list. In the space below, write down a list of all the things that you associate with cowardice.

____

____

____

____

<u>Continue</u>

3. Envy is the third emotion listed in this riddle. In the space below, write down a list of all
   the things that you associate with envy.

____

____

____

4. Now, look at all the lists you have written above. Did you list any colors? What were they?
   If not, list the colors here that you associate most closely with these emotions.

Anger → ____

Cowardice → ____

Emvy → ____

5. Look at the list of colors you just made. What do you associate with all three of these
   colors?

____

6. What is the answer to this riddle?

Answer: ______________________________

<u>Starts with a Y</u>

Starts with a Y
That holds a rock band
That holds the stones
Sent forth by hand.

Figuring it out!

Complete the items below:

1. The first line of this riddle says "Starts with a Y." But "Y" here is not the letter of the alphabet, it is actually a shape. Think of things that have this shape. In the space below, write down things you can think of that are shaped like the letter Y.

____

____

____

2. The second line of this riddle says "That holds a rock band." In this case, though, the "rock band" is not the kind that you would see at a rock concert. What else could these words mean? In the space below write down a list of possible meanings for the words rock band.

____

____

____

<u>Continue</u>

3. The third line of this riddle says "That holds the stones." Think of things that can do the job of holding stones. In the space below, write down a list of things that could be used to hold stones.

____

____

____

4. The last line says "Sent forth by hand." The hand in this line is sending forth the stones from the line above. Think about what this could mean. In the space below, write down a list of your ideas about what it could mean to send forth "stones" by hand.

____

____

____

5. Look at what you have written above. The answer to this riddle is some kind of contraption that looks like a Y that is attached to a band that sends forth stones.

Did you figure it out? If so, what is the answer to this riddle?

Answer: _______________________________

Five Points

I once was a great mausoleum,
But, cursed, I became a museum.
And betwixt my points, five,
Some were buried alive.
Now others line up just to see 'em.

Figuring it out!

The speaker of this riddle is an inanimate object, but it is describing itself. This is an example of an "I am" type of riddle. In order to solve this type of riddle, one needs to figure out what is being self-described by the speaker.

Complete the items below:

1. The first line uses the word "mausoleum." A mausoleum can be described as a type of tomb, perhaps a monument to honor the dead who are laid to rest there. In the space below make a list of any of the famous mausoleums or tombs of which you are aware. If you like, you can begin your list with "Grant's tomb."

Continue

2. In line two, this mausoleum claims to have been "cursed."   The kind of curse being discussed here is a wish that something bad will happen to someone else. If the wish is against you, then you are cursed. Think about all the curses you may have heard about. In the space below write down as many of these as you can remember. If you like, you may start your list with "A witch's curse."

____

____

____

3. The mausoleum that is "speaking" this riddle claims that some were buried alive "…betwixt my points, five." The word "betwixt" basically means the same thing as "between." So, this means that some were buried alive between the mausoleum's five points. A triangle has three points. In the space below write down a list of geometric shapes. Hint—don't limit yourself to two dimensional shapes.

____

____

____

Look at the list you just wrote. Do any of these shapes have exactly five points?

4. Did you figure out what this mausoleum is?

If so, what is the answer to this riddle? ______________________________

<u>Five Lines</u>

A plate upon which no one dines
In a diamond that never shines.
A place to store
More plans for war,
Described by just five lines.

Figuring it out!

The answer to this riddle is a single word, but there are three different major clues in the poem that will help you figure out the answer.

Complete the items below:

1. The first major clue is in the first two lines. The key words are "plate" and "diamond." The plate is not the kind that is used to serve food, and the diamond is not the shiny kind. In the spaces below, first write a list of all the different types of plates you can think of, and then write a list of everything you can associate with the word "diamond."

Plate → ____

____

____

Diamond → ____

____

____

<u>Continue</u> ⇒

2. The second major clue is in lines 3 and 4. "A place to store more plans for war." What could that mean? Where does one store war plans? In the space below write down some of the things you know about planning for war.

____

____

____

3. The third major clue is in line five. "Described by just five lines." While it is true that this riddle is five lines long, and that those lines are a description of sorts, this is not the only meaning of these words. Another kind of line is a straight line that you can draw. In the box below, draw a picture of something, but only use five lines to do it.

4. Look at what you drew.

Can you describe what you drew in one word? ________________________

5. Did you figure it out?

If so, what is the answer to this riddle? _________________________

<u>Riddle Me This</u>

Riddle me this.
Answer me try.
Brother of who, when, where, and why.
What is my name?
What can I be?
I told you! Now you tell me!

Figuring it out!

Complete the items below:

1. In this riddle, the speaker claims to be the brother of *who, when, where,* and *why*. Brothers often share some kind of family resemblance. How do these four words, these "brothers," resemble each other? In the space below, write down any similarities you notice between the words **who**, **when**, **where** and **why**:

____

____

____

2. Who? When? Where? Why? These are examples of question words sometimes called WH words. Often they are grouped together with "How?" Newspaper reporters are trained to answer these questions in their articles when writing a story. In the lines below, write down as many WH question words as you can think of:

____

____

____

<u>Continue</u> ⟹

3. Look at the list you just wrote. Are there any words on that list that are not Who? When? Where? or Why? If so, write just those words in the space below.

____

____

4. A good hint for this riddle is "What is the answer to this riddle." Notice that this hint does *not* have question mark even though it sounds like a question. If this hint is not a question, then what else can the hint mean? In the space below, rephrase the hint but be careful not to turn it into a question:

____

____

5. Did you figure it out?

   If so, what is the answer to this riddle? _______________________________

<u>Upon My Perch</u>

Relaxed I sit upon my perch,
'Til suddenly I give a lurch.
And off I speed on wing-tips three
Before my prey can think to flee.
I make its flesh and tendons part
And claw my way into its heart.

Figuring it out!

Complete the items below:

1. In this riddle, the speaker claims to have three wingtips. Wingtips sometimes have feathers. Birds have two wingtips. There are no birds with three wingtips. The speaker of the riddle cannot be a bird even though it has a perch and claw. In the space below, write down anything you can think of that has three wingtips.

____

____

____

2. Birds of prey do attack small animals and do damage to them with their claws. However, since the answer to the riddle is not a bird, but still it attacks its prey very swiftly and penetrates even to the heart, it is a deadly opponent. Think of things that are not birds, but can still be very fast and deadly. Write a list of these things in the space below.

____

____

____

Continue

3. Look at the list you just wrote. Are all items on your list living things? What if the answer
   to the riddle is not a living thing? Can you think of non-living fast and deadly things? If
   so, write a short list of these things in the space below.

____

____

____

4. Are there any things on the lists you wrote above that fly through the air? The speaker of
   the riddle sits on a perch, then speeds towards its prey using three wingtips. What non-
   living, deadly things fly through the air using three feathers?

____

____

____

5. Did you figure it out? If so, what is the answer to this riddle?

Answer: _____________________________

Inside a Pod

One that rests inside a pod
The one of us not I
Place the ball before you shoot
A drink that's sometimes high

Not who or what, where, when or how
A bee could name me now.

Figuring it out!

This is an unusual riddle because it is really a combination of many small riddles. In order to solve it, you will need to solve a number of small riddles and then put those answers together to solve the whole riddle. The answer you are looking for is a single word.

Complete the items below:

1. The first clue is "one who rests inside a pod." In the space below, write down anything you can associate with the word "pod."

2. The second clue is "The one of us not I." If there are two of us, which is the one of us that is not I?

3. The third clue is "place the ball before you shoot." Think of all the games you can where you need to do this. Make a list of the places where you need to place a ball.

<u>Continue</u>

4. The fourth clue is "A drink that is sometimes high." Can you think of any drinks where people use the word "high" to name them? List any you can think of in the space below.

____

____

____

5. The fifth clue is "Not who or what, where, when or how." What question words are missing from this list? Write them in the space below.

____

6. The last line says that "A bee can name me now." But this bee is not an insect that flies around to collect pollen. How many other kinds of bees are there? Write down as many as you can think of in the space below.

____

____

7. Now, look at all the answers you gave for 1 – 5 above. Are there any similar kinds of answers? Do any of the answers you gave sound like the names of letters of the alphabet? If so, write those words here.

____

8. Did you figure it out?

   If so, what is the answer to this riddle? _______________________________

Dormitory

It's clear a dormitory
Is indeed a dirty room
And that a schoolmaster
Matches the classroom.
But did you know a funeral
Is a form of real fun?
And that eleven plus two
Is the same as twelve plus one?

Figuring it out!

Complete the items below:

This riddle is made up of four clues. Each clue is two lines long. The third clue does not seem to make much logical sense. Not many people think that having a funeral is fun, and yet the riddle tells us that "...a funeral is a form of real fun". Since an actual funeral is not fun, let's instead, turn this into an equation. The equation for clue #3 is:

(Clue #3) **Funeral = Real fun**

Help make the equations for the other three clues by filling out the blank spaces below:

(Clue #1) Dormitory   = _______________________________________

(Clue #2) Schoolmaster = _______________________________________

Clue #4) Eleven plus two = _______________________________________

<u>Continue</u> ⟹

Look at what you just did. Did you write the numerals "12 + 1," or did you write out the words "twelve plus one"? Since the riddle uses the words, you should too. In the space below, write down any similarities you see between the words on the left side of each equation and the words on the right hand side. (Hint: How many times does the letter "w" appear?)

____

____

____

____

Did you figure it out? If so, describe what you notice about each of the four clues, or if you know it, write the one-word answer to the riddle?

One-word answer :   _________________________________

Or description:

____

____

____

____

____

The Hunter

The hunter far and wide will roam,
Like a ghost of sun and shadow.
First she'll brush then find the comb,
And then put on a dancing show.
Mother waits inside her home,
Where golden treasure flows.

Figuring it out!

Complete the items below:

1. In this riddle, the hunter is like "a ghost of sun and shadow." To help figure out what the hunter is like, we should consider what the sun is like and what a shadow is like. In the spaces below, write down things that you associate with "sun" and "shadow."

Sun→

____

____

Shadow→

____

____

2. The third line mentions a "comb" and a "brush." These words have nothing to do with styling hair. In the spaces below write down as many meanings of these words as you can.

Brush→

____

Continue ⟹

Comb→

3. In the last two lines, the mother is waiting in a special home. This is a home where "golden treasure" flows. Who lives in a home with golden treasure? Why does it flow? Water flows, but gold coins do not. In the lines below write down other things that flow.

Look at the list you just wrote. Are any of these things "golden" in color?

4. Putting it all together. From the sun and shadow clues did you write down their colors? What are they? What else has these colors? What is it with these colors that needs to find a comb (different from a hair comb)? Who is the female who waits in this "hunter's" home among the flowing golden treasure? You may use the lines below to help you gather your thoughts.

Colors of sun and shadow? _______________________________________

Kind of comb? _______________________________________

Who waits at home? _______________________________________

5. Did you figure out who the hunter is?

If so, what is the answer to this riddle? _______________

<u>The Ballet</u>

I start off the ballet.
I'm a dance. I'm a room.
I can also be found in
A circus balloon.
If you're having fun,
You might have one of me.
Hard, soft and basket;
Foot, base and tee.

Figuring it out!

Complete the items below:

1. In this riddle, the speaker claims to be associated with many things. Of the four clues in the first four lines (ballet, dance, room, and circus balloon) two of them (ballet and circus balloon) are what we will call CLUE TYPE 1. In the spaces below write these two clues.

CLUE TYPE 1 ______________________________   ______________________________

  Look at what you just wrote. Do you notice any similarities between these two clues?

2. "Dance" is an example of a different kind of clue. Call this CLUE TYPE 2. In the space below write down the names of different kinds of dances.

CLUE TYPE 2— DANCE

____

____

____

<u>Continue</u>

3. In the second half of this riddle, there is a CLUE TYPE 2 (having fun). Another way to say having fun is to say "I'm having a good time." or "I'm having a blast." In the space below, write down different ways of saying "having fun."

CLUE TYPE 2—HAVING FUN

____

____

____

4. The riddle also contains seven examples of CLUE TYPE 3. The words room, hard, soft, basket, foot, base, and tee are all parts of different compound words. If you join the word "school" to the word "house" you get the compound word "schoolhouse." The CLUE TYPE 3 words are each one part of a compound word. The other part of the compound is the same across all seven clue words. It can go either before or after the clue words (example: foot_____). In the spaces below write as many compound words as you can think of using these seven clues.

CLUE TYPE 3—COMPOUNDS

____

____

____

____

5. Did you figure it out? If so, what is the answer to this riddle?

Answer: ____

A Dozen Royals

A dozen Royals gathered round,
Entertained by two who clowned.

Each King there had servants ten,
Though none of them were also men.

The lowest servant sometimes might,
Defeat the King in a fair fight.

A weapon stout, a priceless jewel,
The beat of life, a farmer's tool.

Figuring it out!

This riddle is a description of several aspects of the same thing. This thing has several components, but the answer to the riddle is really only one thing that names the entire collection.

Complete the items below:

To get a general idea of how many things are in this collection, study the poem to find some numbers. Answer each of the following questions with a number:

1. How many "Royals" are there? _______________________________________

2. How many clowns are there? _____________________________________

3. How many servants does each king have? _____________________________

4. The riddle does not say how many of these royals actually are kings, but at least some of them are. Answer this yes/no question. According to the riddle, is there more than one king? _____________

5. Assume that the *clowns* are not also *servants* or *royals*. If so, then at a minimum, there are ***at least*** how many things total in this collection? ________________

Continue

Questions 6 – 9 are based on the list found in the last two lines of the riddle.

6. Make a list of all the stout, handheld weapons you can think of.

____

____

7. Make a list of all the valuable jewels you can think of.

____

____

8. What is the beat of life? List your ideas about what this phrase might mean.

____

____

9. List as many farmers' tools as you can think of.

____

____

10. Look for relationships between things on your lists above. Did you figure it out? If so, what is the answer to this riddle?

Answer: _______________________________________

The Prisoner

A prisoner he might appear,
Not gagged but strongly bound.
Forced to tell his tale again,
He does and makes no sound.
His questioner just sits and stares
And nothing's ever heard.
He's then released because, in truth,
He's told them every word.

Figuring it out!

Complete the items below:

1. In this riddle the prisoner is not gagged, and yet he tells his tale without making a sound. He communicates every word of his story without ever talking or being talked to. This is very strange. Maybe the prisoner is not a person. In the space below, write a list of ways to communicate a story without speaking.

____

____

____

2. The riddle says that the prisoner is "strongly bound." If it were a person, one could imagine that the prisoner's hands were tied together, and that maybe he is also tied to a chair or a wall. But if the prisoner is not a person, then "bound" might mean something different from tying a rope around something. In the space below write down all the meanings of the word "bound" that you can think of.

____

____

____

Continue ⇨

3. If someone releases a prisoner, then he or she might untie the person and let him go. But, if this prisoner is not a person, then maybe there is another way to "release" the prisoner. In the space below, write down different meanings of the word "release."

____

____

____

4. Now, look at all the lists you have written above. If the prisoner is not a person, what can it be?

5. Did you figure it out? If so, what is the answer to this riddle?

Answer: ____

<u>The Snake</u>

The snake can't ever make them
The shark he never tries,
The eagle prefers not to,
And so away he flies.

And yet one always finds them
In many climes and lands,
A man himself can make them
But never with his hands.

Figuring it out!

This riddle is about the nature of something. The various clues tell you things that are true about the answer. The trouble is that most of the clues are negative which means they tell you what this thing is not. These pages will help you if you have not already figured out the answer.

Complete the items below:

Continue ⟹

1. The riddle talks about a snake, a shark, and an eagle. First draw a picture of these three animals in the box below.

2. Whatever they are, the riddle says that the snake can't make them, and the shark never tries. But it also says that the eagle prefers not to. This means that the eagle could make them if he wanted to. Look at the pictures you just drew, and think about the differences between these three animals. In the space below, write down all the ways that an eagle is different from the other two animals.

____

____

____

3. In the last part of the riddle, it says that man himself can make them but never with his hands. Think about things you can make without using your hands. In the space below, write down anything you can think of that you can make without using your hands.

____

____

____

4. You can make them, an eagle can make them, but a snake can't. What are they? Did you figure it out?

If so, what is the answer to this riddle? _______________________________________

Steadfast Mates

You'd think their marriage terribly marred,
She so sharp, and he so hard.

And their union doubtless flawed,
Her end pointed, his end clawed.

His every action appears abuse,
As he strikes and strikes her without truce.

But each, to the other, a steadfast mate,
That, in their congress, goods create.

For each is useless when alone,
But both in tandem build a home.

Figuring it out!

The answer to this riddle is not really a married couple, but instead it is a pair of inanimate objects.

Complete the items below:

1. In this riddle the husband is described as having an end that is clawed. He is also described as hard. Think of things that are hard and things that have a clawed end. Write down a list of things that have one, the other, or both of these characteristics.

____

____

____

Continue ⇒

2. In this riddle the wife is described as having a pointed end. She is also described as sharp.
   Think of things that are sharp and pointed. Write down a list of things that have these
   characteristics.

____

____

____

3. This husband and wife team built a home. Since they are not people, this does not mean
   that they are interested in the warm and welcoming aspects of a home. Instead it means
   that they literally built a house. In the space below list things that you might use to build
   a house.

____

____

____

4. Now look at the lists you have written above. If the husband and wife are not people, what
   can they be? Did you figure it out? If so, what is the answer to this riddle?

If so, what is the answer to this riddle? ____________________________________

<u>Hidden Weapon</u>

Stars awash in sheen of light
It calls out loud in vile delight.
Listeners endure in fright.
Vicious brute that reigns at night,
Evil whelped of heinous bite,
Renewed by wax, it gains in might.

A leading way to slay the beast,
Thus hidden weapon is released.

Figuring it out!

Complete the items below:

1. The first six lines of this riddle describe a particular kind of beast. The riddle is set at night and one of the things the beast does is to call out loud. In the space below write down a list of animals that you can think of that make night noises.

2. Line six says "Renewed by wax, it gains in might." This means that the beast gets stronger because of wax. But "wax" in this case is not candle wax or beeswax. In the space below write down other meaning of wax.

<u>Continue</u>

3. Line five says "Evil whelped of heinous bite." This means that the beast was born because something was bitten. In the space below write down anything you can think of that this line reminds you of.

____

____

____

4. The last two lines talk about the hidden weapon that can slay the beast. The weapon is hidden in the first six lines of this riddle in a leading way. What do you notice about the first part of every line in the first six lines? Write down the capital letters of these lines here.

____

5. What you just wrote down might be the weapon used to slay the beast. What is the beast?

Answer: _______________________________

<u>Mates</u>

Mates unbalanced,
Or so they seem;
But paired in tandem,
A deadly team.

She so gently rounded,
He so firm and straight,
Yet when they are compounded,
Woe to them they hate.

Figuring it out!

Complete the items below:

1. In this riddle, the answer is actually two things instead of just one. They are paired as part of a team. These are things that commonly go together like peanut-butter and jelly or salt and pepper.   In the space below, write a list of things that commonly go together:

____

____

____

Look at what you just wrote. Are any of these things "deadly"?

<u>Continue</u> ⇨

2. The two team members in this riddle are very different from each other. "She" is described as gently rounded. "He" is described as firm and straight. But the two things that make up the answer are not people or animals. Instead they are inanimate objects. In the spaces below write a list of things you can think of that are rounded, and then a list of things that are firm and straight.

Rounded →
____

Straight →
____

____

3. These two things form a "deadly team." Neither one alone is very dangerous, but when used together they can be deadly. In the space below, write a list of things that you can think of that are deadly.

____

____

Look at what you just wrote. Are any of these deadly things made up of two parts? Could one part be called rounded while the other part is straight?

4. Did you figure it out? If so, what is the answer to this riddle? ________________________

<u>Do Me In</u>

Do me in to do the law
So you can do me out.
Do me through, do me to ground,
Give me away, you lout.

Do me down or do me up
But up I'll get a heart.
Do me when you are in camp
To get an early start.

Do me fast when I'm the day,
So fast I get a neck.
Do me even, to a horse,
Take five - Oh what the heck.

Figuring it out!

Complete the items below:

1. In this who am I riddle, the answer is a word that can often take the place of the words *do me*. There are 15 words that are clues, but the clues are of different types. In one type of clue, the answer is one part of a compound word. In the spaces below, fill in the blank with any word you can think of that will turn each answer into a regular English compound word. For example, if the clue was "________house" you might write work*house* or you might write play*house*:

________through,

________down,

________up,

________fast,

________neck

Look at the words you just wrote. Could any one of them fit in all the spaces above?

<u>Continue</u> ⟹

2. When people sleep at a campsite during a long hike, they need to pack up before they continue the hike. In the space below, write different ways of describing these actions.

____

____

____

3. When people violate the law, they can get in trouble. In the space below write different ways of saying "violate the law."

____

____

____

4. When people "take five," it means that they take a rest from what they were doing. In the space below, write different ways of saying take a rest.

____

____

____

5. Did you figure it out? If so, what is the answer to this riddle? _______________

<u>My Cross</u>

Since he was cross, and I was cross,
We crossed across the field.
I crossed my cross across his cross
To try to make him yield.

So toe to toe we both did go
And crossed our crosses fell.
When my cross crossed across his cross
It clanged just like a bell.

What is my cross, what is his cross
That crisscrossed through the air?
Now don't get cross if you can't guess.
It is my cross to bare.

Figuring it out!

"What is my cross?" the riddle asks. The answer to this riddle is not a cross. It is something that, in some ways, is like a cross. To answer this riddle correctly you need to figure out what the "cross" really is.

Complete the items below:

1. The word "cross" in the first line means angry or mad. Sometimes you can tell when people are angry by their actions. In the space below write a list of things that people do that show that they are angry.

<u>Continue</u> ⟹

2. The speaker of the poem is trying to make someone else "yield" or give up. The two of
   them ("he" and "I") are in some kind of fight. In the space below make a list of all the
   different ways you can think of that people fight.

____

____

____

3. At the end of the second stanza, the riddle says "When my cross crossed across his cross
   it clanged just like a bell." In the box below, draw a picture of what might be going on.

4. Notice the spelling of "bare" in the last line. To bare something means to uncover it. In
   the space below make a list of all things that you would uncover in order to fight with
   them.

____

____

____

5. Did you figure out what the cross actually is?

If so, what is the answer to this riddle? _______________________

<u>Aphrodite</u>

A gruesome traveler, mud bemired,
Approaches here all worn and tired.
Upon the spot a trim bed makes,
And of her rest she then partakes.
Her silken sheets she wraps so tight,
They quite conceal her from my sight.

Now oft' before I've heard it said,
That beauty marred is healed in bed.
But to me such talk was cheap,
I've not believed in beauty sleep.
Until I saw this traveler wake,
And she her silken bed forsake.
Who went to bed at best untidy,
Arose at length an Aphrodite.

Figuring it out!

Complete the items below:

1. To answer this riddle you need to say who the "gruesome traveler" is. The riddle tells us
   that she arrives and goes to bed in "silken sheets." Why do you suppose the sheets are
   silk? In the space below write down what you know about how silk is made.

____

____

____

<u>Continue</u> ⟹

2. Aphrodite is the name of the Greek goddess of love and beauty. So the riddle tells us that the traveler goes to bed looking gruesome and muddy, but wakes up beautiful. The answer to the riddle is not a person, but is, instead, something found in nature. In the space below write down things you can think of that undergo transformations in nature.

____

____

____

Look at what you just wrote. Do any of these transformations begin ugly, and end up beautiful?

____

3. The riddle tells us that the gruesome traveler wraps her silken sheets in a way that actually conceals her. After she emerges, she is beautiful. Think of a chick emerging from an egg. What other things in nature can you think of that emerge from a hiding place? In the space below, write down a list of the things you can think of in nature that emerge from a tight hiding place.

____

____

____

4. What is the answer to this riddle? _______________________________

<u>Lustrous Beauty</u>

Behold the lustrous beauty of my bride.
The colors of the night shine in her skin.
I long for arms to hold her to my side;
In truth this game is one I ne'er can win.

And wed were we as day turned into night.
She held a pure bouquet of whitest flour.
Her dress was red and I was tawny white.
Our ceremony took but half an hour.

My bride was born to be Baba Ghanoush;
While mother mine was but a lowly cow.
My wife had grown up looking like a bush
So is my bride not known to you by now?

Though she was grown and raised by Farmer John,
Our married surname now is Parmesan.

Figuring it out!

Complete the items below:

1. The answer to this riddle is the name of the bride. But the bride and the bridegroom are not people. Listing things that the riddle tells you about the bridegroom and the bride may help you solve this riddle. In the spaces below list the things the riddle tells you about the bridegroom and the bride.

Bridegroom→
____

Bride→
____

____

<u>Continue</u> ⇒

2. At the end of line six is the word 'flour' instead of the word 'flower.' This word is not a mistake in spelling, instead it tells you a great deal about the nature of the bride and groom. In the space below write down things you associate with the word 'flour'

3. The "wedding" in the riddle is not a real wedding, but it stands for these two objects coming together to form a sort of union. Given what you have written above, what kinds of things are the bride and groom, and what happened during the half-hour wedding?

4. Did you figure out what the bride actually is?

If so, what is the answer to this riddle? ________________________________

<u>The Strange House</u>

This house holds rooms, one score and six,
That shelter a vast mob.
It lets lions lie down with the lambs,
Yet makes both shun the slob.

None now will nestle with nicks and nates,
While reams room near the rear.
Though you and I have separate rooms
Both our bottles brim with beer.

The king and queen can never mate
(Though hands and hearts hobnob)
Because their rooms are separate
If this jail does its job.

What house is this that rules thus
Forcing faith to fend with fear?
The answer to this riddle lies
With dead and dying here.

Figuring it out!

The answer to this riddle is a single, inanimate object with many things inside. Looking at the clues in the riddle will help you figure out what that one thing might be

Complete the items below:

1. The number of rooms in this house is "one score and six." A score is equal to twenty, so this house has twenty-six rooms. What does twenty-six remind you of? In the space below write down a list of things you associate with the number twenty-six.

2. In line three, the strange house "…lets lions lie down with the lambs." What do lions have in common with lambs? In the space below write down everything you think lions and lambs have in common.

Continue ⇨

3. In line five we find that "None now will nestle with nicks and nates," Look at the words in this line. In the space below, write down what many of these words have in common?

____

____

4. In line fourteen, the house is "Forcing faith to fend with fear." Look at the words in this line. In the space below, write down what many of these words have in common?

____

____

5. Look at your responses to items 1-4 above. See if you can find any similarities. Now look at the whole riddle. In the space below, write down any pattern you notice about the words in this riddle that are assigned to the same room in this very strange house.

____

____

6. Did you figure out what this strange house could be?

If so, what is the answer to this riddle? _______________________________

<u>Cyclops</u>

A cyclops stares from pale white face.
Earrings seven his visage grace.
Atop his head are five tattoos.
Ebon black his pair of shoes.

On his pale back six scars dug deep.
He felt no pain and did not weep.
His job to tumble, bounce and fall;
But he's no fool. No not at all!

Figuring it out!

This riddle is an "I saw" riddle. The "cyclops" is being described by the speaker of the riddle, but the cyclops himself is not the speaker. The thing being described is actually an inanimate object that in some ways is like a cyclops. The job of the solver of the riddle is to figure out what is really being described here.

Complete the items below:

There are quite a few numbers that are in this riddle. Some of the obvious ones are seven, five, and six, but there are other numbers implied. Even though a cyclops has **one** eye, he probably has **two** ears, so when you fill in the numbers below, divide the earrings in such a way as they are not all on one ear. In each space below, write in one numeral that you think best answers the question:

1. How many eyes does the cyclops have? ___________

2. How many shoes does the cyclops have? ___________

3. How many earrings are on the cyclops' left ear? ___________

4. How many earrings are on the cyclops' right ear? ___________

5. How many tattoos are on the cyclops' head? ___________

6. How many scars are on the cyclops' back? ___________

<u>Continue</u>

7. The riddle uses the word "pale" twice. First describing the cyclops' face, and then describing his back. Considering these clues, guess the color of the cyclops' skin.

____

8. The riddle also uses the phrase "ebon black" when describing the shoes. If we extend this idea to include everything else, what color would all these items be?

____

9. Draw the cyclops as described in this poem:

10. Did you figure it out what the cyclops actually is?

   If so, what is the answer to this riddle? _________________________________

INDEX

Note: The bold numbers indicate the page containing the best example of that concept.

Alphabetical Index of Educational Concepts

Categorical Index of Educational Concepts

Aspects of English Grammar

Figurative Language

Poetic Conventions and Techniques

Riddle Conventions

Verse Forms

Don't forget to visit our web site at www.CloudKingdom.com for the free riddle of the week, discussions of using riddles and puzzles in a classroom and to see our other riddle books.

www.ingramcontent.com/pod-product-compliance
Lightning Source LLC
Chambersburg PA
CBHW080346030726